THE BIG FIGHT QUIZ

THE BIG FIGHT QUIZ BOOK

COMPILED BY
NORMAN GILLER

ILLUSTRATED BY
DAVID EDWARDS

REFEREED BY ITV'S
VOICE OF BOXING
REG GUTTERIDGE

Robson Books

Acknowledgements

Norman Giller, deviser and compiler of *The Big Fight Quiz Book*, wishes to thank Jeremy Robson and his editorial team for their encouragement, Michael Giller for his Apple-a-day computer talent, artist David Edwards for his graphic support, and the doyen of ringside commentators, Reg Gutteridge, for his refereeing role. Nobody can compile a book like this without bowing the knee to the two bibles of boxing, *The Ring Magazine* and *Boxing News*. I also dipped freely into the waters of knowledge that flow through the pages of Harry Mullan's authoritative *Illustrated History of Boxing*, various volumes of Barry J. Hugman's *British Boxing Year Book*, plus his excellent *Boxing Monthly*, and, naturally, my old workmate Ron Olver's always-informative Old-Timers' column in *Boxing News*.

First published in Great Britain in 1989 by Robson Books Limited
Bolsover House, 5-6 Clipstone Street, London W1P 7EB

British Library Cataloguing in Publication Data
   Giller, Norman
   The Big Fight Quiz Book.
   1. Boxing
   I. Title
   796.8'3

ISBN 0 86051 614 8

Typeset and designed by Norman Giller Enterprises, Shoeburyness, Essex, England

Printed in Great Britain by T.J. Press (Padstow) Ltd, Padstow, Cornwall.

CONTENTS

Seconds out

Reg Gutteridge
ITV's Voice of Boxing

No matter where I go in the world in search of ring action ('Have mike, will travel') there is always some clever Dick waiting to try to floor me with a question about boxing. Of all the sports, none attracts the record fanatic quite like the fight game. Well, here's a book that will keep the mind and the memory of even the most fervent boxing buff working overtime for hours on end.

I am here in the role of referee to see that we have a good, clean quiz contest. There are 15 rounds of questions on each of 75 of the greatest champions of the century, going back to magnificent old timers like Ted 'Kid' Lewis, Jack Dempsey and Gene Tunney, and coming up to date with tests on modern masters like Sugar Ray Leonard, Mike Tyson, Frank Bruno and Nigel Benn.

There is a scorecard check at the end of each challenge, and you will find the answers to each quiz on the next page but one. Keep a tally of your points score, and when you have gone the distance across a marathon of 1,125 questions you will be able to gauge your all-round boxing knowledge by checking your score with a ratings table on page 160. When you are struggling to come up with the answer there is an 'a-b-c' selection to trigger your memory, and, perhaps, to help you make an educated guess.

You are in expert hands with the questionmaster, Norman Giller. Since starting on the journalistic ladder as my copyboy on the late, lamented London *Evening News* some 35 years ago he has gone on to become one of the leading freelance sportswriters in the land. He was a staffman on *Boxing News*, the *Daily Herald* and the *Daily Express* before tunnelling his way out of Fleet Street to set up in business on his own. The 30-plus sports books that he has had published include collaborations on boxing tomes with Henry

Cooper, Frank Bruno and my ringside partner, Jim Watt; he was also my co-author on an early biography of 'Iron' Mike Tyson. Twelve of his books have been written in partnership with his long-time pal Jimmy Greaves, who used to be a regular ringside supporter of boxing in his days as a jinking genius of the football pitch.

Norman—like a moth, he is in to everything—was employed as a publicist on the Muhammad Ali-Richard Dunn and Frank Bruno-Tim Witherspoon world heavyweight title fights, and he banged the drum for domestic classics such as Dave (Boy) Green v. John H. Stracey, Alan Minter v. Chris Finnegan and Herol (Bomber) Graham v. Mark Kaylor. He works extensively in television, and he is a regular member of the *This Is Your Life* team. He scripted the programmes featuring boxing idols Jack (Kid) Berg, Barry McGuigan and his close friend, Terry Lawless.

It was Norman who devised ITV's popular series, *Who's the Greatest?*, of which the highlight was the boxing battle between Muhammad Ali and Rocky Marciano. I was a witness for Ali on that show in which Dennis Waterman put an eloquent case for Muhammad against a spirited defence of Marciano by that master wordsmith Eamonn Andrews. Ali quite rightly won it, and, in my opinion, he remains—alongside Sugar Ray Robinson—'The Greatest.' Both Ali and the original Sugar Ray naturally feature in the following pages.

Norman and his chip-off-the-block son, Michael, devised this Big Fight Quiz challenge and they compiled it with the devilish help of their wizard computers. In the introduction to each quiz you will find how many questions you need to answer correctly to win by a knock out or on points.

That's enough of the pre-fight instructions. Now it's 'seconds out' for the first round. Good luck, and come out answering...

Reg Gutteridge

THE BIG FIGHT QUIZ No. 1

IN THIS CORNER

Muhammad Ali

Award yourself a points win if you get eight or more right. It's a draw if you get seven right. You win by a knockout if you get 12 or more right.

1 At which Olympics did the then Cassius Clay win a gold medal at light-heavyweight? a) Rome 1960; b) Tokyo 1964; c) Mexico 1968

2 Which former world champion did he beat in four rounds in his 16th fight? a) Joey Maxim; b) Harold Johnson; c) Archie Moore

3 In which round did he stop Henry Cooper in their non-title contest at Wembley Stadium in 1963? a) Fourth round; b) Fifth round; c) Sixth round

4 Who was the first opponent to force Ali (then Clay) to take a count? a) Sonny Banks; b) Willi Besmanoff; c) Henry Cooper

5 Where did he make his first challenge for the world heavyweight title? a) Atlantic City; b) Los Angeles; c) Miami Beach

6 At the end of which round did Sonny Liston retire in their first championship contest? a) Fifth round; b) Sixth round; c) Seventh round

7 In which round did Joe Frazier knock Ali down in their first title fight? a) Eleventh round; b) Thirteenth round; c) Fifteenth round

8 Against which opponent did Ali suffer a broken jaw in a non-title fight? a) Earnie Shavers; b) Ken Norton; c) Jimmy Young

10

How many contests did Ali have during his professional career? a) 61; b) 71; c) 81

 In which year did he have his final fight? a) 1979; b) 1981; c) 1983

 Where was he born? a) St Louis; b) Louisiana; c) Louisville

 Who was his opponent when his trainer Angelo Dundee worked in the opposite corner? a) Doug Jones; b) Jimmy Ellis; c) Zora Folley

 Where did he defend his world championship against Joe Bugner in 1975? a) Nova Scotia; b) Manila; c) Kuala Lumpur

 Who did he beat in a world championship fight in New Orleans? a) Ron Lyle; b) Alfredo Evangelista; c) Leon Spinks

 Against which opponent did he have the final contest of his career? a) Larry Holmes; b) Trevor Berbick; c) Jean Pierre Coopman

BIG FIGHT QUIZ ANSWERS

The answers to this Muhammad Ali quiz appear on the next page but one. Award yourself one point for each question that you answer correctly. On page 160 there is a table that gauges how you rate with your boxing knowledge, based on your total points score.

SCORECARD

Points:

Result:

IN THIS CORNER

Dennis Andries

Award yourself a points win if you get seven or more right. It's a draw if you get six right. You win by a knockout if you get 11 or more right.

1 In which country was Dennis Andries born?
a) Jamaica; b) Guyana; c) St Kitts

2 Which former British heavyweight champion outpointed him in his ninth fight? a) Bunny Johnson; b) Neville Meade; c) John L. Gardner

3 In which district of London was he based before moving to the United States? a) Canning Town; b) Hackney; c) Elephant and Castle

4 Who beat him on points in a fight for the vacant British light-heavyweight title in 1982? a) Tom Collins; b) Tim Wood; c) Trevor Cattouse

5 In which round did he knock out Devon Bailey in defence of his British light-heavyweight title in 1984? a) Eighth round; b) Tenth; c) Twelfth round

6 What was the nationality of Alex Blanchard, with whom he drew in a European title fight in 1985? a) French; b) Dutch; c) Belgian

7 Where did he make his first challenge for the world championship in 1986? a) Watford; b) Edmonton; c) Finsbury Park

8 From whom did he take the WBC world light-heavyweight title in 1986? a) J.B. Williamson; b) Dwight Braxton; c) Marvin Johnson

12

In which year did he make his professional debut? a) 1976; b) 1978; c) 1980

 He became world champion after how many contests? a) 25; b) 35; c) 45

 Who did he stop in his first world title defence ? a) Tony Sibson; b) Leslie Stewart; c) Bobby Czyz

ANDRIES

 In which round did Tommy Hearns stop him in their world championship fight in 1987? a) Tenth round; b) Eleventh round; c) Twelfth round

 Dennis based himself in which American city after losing his title to Hearns? a) Philadelphia; b) San Francisco; c) Detroit

 Who was the American who took over as his manager in the United States? a) Emanuel Steward; b) Eddie Futch; c) Butch Lewis

 Who did he stop in five rounds to regain the WBC world light-heavyweight title in 1989? a) Donnie Lalonde; b) Virgil Hill; c) Tony Willis

BIG FIGHT QUIZ No 1 ANSWERS

MUHAMMAD ALI: 1. Rome, 1960; 2. Archie Moore; 3. Fifth round; 4. Sonny Banks; 5. Miami Beach; 6. Sixth round; 7. Fifteenth round; 8. Ken Norton; 9. 61 contests; 10. 1981; 11. Louisville; 12. Jimmy Ellis; 13. Kuala Lumpur; 14. Leon Spinks; 15. Trevor Berbick.

SCORECARD

Points:

Result:

IN THIS CORNER
Henry Armstrong

Award yourself a points win if you get six or more right. It's a draw if you get five right. You win by a knockout if you get ten or more right.

1 How many world titles did Armstrong hold simultaneously? a) Two; b) Three; c) Four

2 At which weight did he win his first world championship? a) Bantamweight; b) Featherweight; c) Lightweight

3 Which famous singer spotted his potential and helped him find a manager? a) Bing Crosby; b) Rudy Vallee; c) Al Jolson

4 What was his real surname under which he made his professional debut? a) Jackson; b) Dobson; c) Atkinson

5 By what popular nickname was he best known? a) Henry The Hammer; b) Homicide Hank; c) Motion 'n' Commotion

6 Which great fighter did he beat to become world welterweight champion in 1938? a) Tony Canzoneri; b) Jimmy McLarnin; c) Barney Ross

7 In which round did he knock out Petey Sarron to become undisputed world featherweight champion? a) Second round; b) Fourth round; c) Sixth round

8 Against which opponent did Armstrong defend his welterweight title in London in 1939? a) Ernie Roderick; b) Eric Boon; c) Jake Kilrain

14

How many contests did he have during his professional career?
a) 101; b) 141; c) 181

 In which year did he have his final fight?
a) 1945; b) 1943; c) 1941

 In which American town was he born?
a) Columbus, Mississippi; b) New Orleans, Louisiana; c) Birmingham, Alabama

 Who was his opponent when he was held to a draw bidding for the middleweight title? a) Ceferino Garcia; b) Ken Overlin; c) Solly Kreiger

 How many fights did he have in his busiest year of 1937, winning them all and with only one going the distance?
a)19; b) 23; c) 27

 Who beat him in his last fight, four weeks after holding him to a draw? a) Genaro Rojo; b) Chester Slider; c) Ray Robinson

What did he become after hanging up his gloves?
a) A preacher; b) A promoter; c) A cotton farmer

BIG FIGHT QUIZ No 2 ANSWERS

DENNIS ANDRIES: 1.Guyana; 2. Bunny Johnson; 3. Hackney; 4. Tom Collins; 5. Twelfth round; 6. Dutch; 7. Edmonton; 8. J.B. Williamson; 9. 1978; 10. 35 contests; 11. Tony Sibson; 12. Tenth round; 13. Detroit; 14. Emanuel Steward; 15. Tony Willis.

SCORECARD

Points:

Result:

THE BIG FIGHT QUIZ No. 4

IN THIS CORNER

Carmen Basilio

Award yourself a points win if you get seven or more right. It's a draw if you get six right. You win by a knockout if you get 11 or more right.

1 How old was Basilio when he made his professional debut in 1948? a) 17; b) 19; c) 21

2 He was born in Canastota, but was billed from which town when fighting? a) Syracuse; b) Toledo; c) Buffalo

3 On what sort of farm did he work before becoming a full-time professional? a) A potato farm; b) An onion farm; c) A pig farm

4 Who beat him when he first fought for the undisputed world welterweight title? a) Kid Gavilan; b) Marty Servo; c) Billy Graham

5 Who did he twice stop in 12 rounds in world welterweight champion contests? a) Tommy Bell; b) Tony De Marco; c) Art Aragon

6 In which round did he knock out Johnny Saxton in their third world welterweight title fight? a) Sixth round; b) Fourth round; c) Second round

7 Which former world lightweight champion did he outpoint over 10 rounds in 1953? a) Ike Williams; b) Jimmy Carter; c) Wallace (Bud) Smith

8 In which year did he first challenge Sugar Ray Robinson for the world middleweight championship? a) 1957; b) 1956; c) 1958

How many contests did Basilio have during his career? a) 79; b) 99; c) 89

 In which year did he have his final fight? a) 1963; b) 1961; c) 1965

 How many times was he beaten? a) 16; b) 12; c) 8

 How many times did he fight Sugar Ray Robinson? a) Twice; b) Three times; c) Four times

 In which round was he stopped by Gene Fullmer in their first world title fight? a) Seventh round; b) Tenth round; c) Fourteenth round

 Which former world welterweight champion did he beat in his last fight but one? a) Don Jordan; b) Benny (Kid) Paret; c) Virgil Akins

 Against which champion did he make a bid to regain the middleweight title in his last fight? a) Carl (Bobo) Olson; b) Paul Pender; c) Dick Tiger

BIG FIGHT QUIZ No 3 ANSWERS

HENRY ARMSTRONG: 1. Three; 2. Featherweight; 3. Al Jolson; 4. Jackson; 5. Homicide Hank; 6. Barney Ross; 7. Sixth round; 8. Ernie Roderick; 9. 181 fights; 10. 1945; 11. Columbus; 12. Ceferino Garcia; 13. 27 fights; 14. Chester Slider; 15. A preacher.

SCORECARD

Points:

Result:

THE BIG FIGHT QUIZ No. 5

IN THIS CORNER

Nigel Benn

Award yourself a points win if you get eight or more right. It's a draw if you get seven right. You win by a knockout if you get 12 or more right.

1 Nigel Benn was serving with which branch of the armed forces when he first took up boxing? a) Royal Navy; b) Royal Air Force; c) Army

2 With which club was he an outstanding amateur boxer? a) Fitzroy Lodge; b) West Ham; c) Repton

3 At which weight did he win an ABA title the year before turning professional? a) Welterweight; b) Light-middleweight; c) Middleweight

4 Who was his manager when he first turned professional? a) Burt McCarthy; b) Terry Lawless; c) Frank Warren

5 What is his popular nickname? a) The Black Bomber; b) The Dark Destroyer; c) The Black Assassin

6 Reggie Miller was the first opponent to take him past four rounds. How many rounds did he survive? a) Six; b) Seven; c) Eight

7 At which venue did he become Commonwealth middleweight champion in 1988? a) Royal Albert Hall; b) Alexandra Palace c) Finsbury Park

8 Against which opponent did he win the vacant Commonwealth championship? a) Umaru Sanda; b) Graeme Ahmed; c) Byron Price

In which year was he born?
a) 1962; b) 1964; c) 1966

 Where was he born?
a) Ilford; b) Sydenham;
c) Paddington

 Who is his trainer?
a) Jimmy Tibbs; b) Brian
Lynch; c) Ernie Fossey

 Against which opponent did he get off the canvas to win in
1988? a) Tim Williams; b) Anthony Logan; c) Darren
Hobson

 In which round did he knock out Mike Chilambe in defence
of his Commonwealth championship in 1989?
a) First; b) Second; c) Third

 In which city did he knock out Mbayo Wa Mbayo in 1989?
a) Manchester; b) Birmingham; c) Glasgow

 Who was the promoter of his showdown with Michael
Watson in May, 1989? a) Mike Barrett; b) Frank Warren;
c) Frank Maloney.

BIG FIGHT QUIZ No 4 ANSWERS

CARMEN BASILIO: 1. 21 years old; 2. Syracuse; 3.
Onion farm; 4. Kid Gavilan; 5. Tony De Marco; 6.
Second round; 7. Ike Williams; 8. 1957; 9. 79 contests;
10. 1961; 11. 16 times; 12. Twice; 13. 14th round; 15.
Don Jordan; 15. Paul Pender.

SCORECARD

Points:

Result:

IN THIS CORNER

Nino Benvenuti

Award yourself a points win if you get six or more right. It's a draw if you get five right. You win by a knockout if you get 10 or more right.

1 At which Olympics did Nino Benvenuti win an Olympic gold medal? a) Rome 1960; b) Tokyo 1964; c) Melbourne 1956

2 He was Olympic champion at which weight? a) Light-welterweight; b) Welterweight; c) Light-middle-weight

3 In which round did he stop his first British opponent, George Aldridge, in Rome in 1962? a) Sixth round; b) Eighth round; c) Tenth round

4 From which of his fellow-countrymen did he win the world light-middleweight title? a) Sandro Mazzinghi; b) Carmelo Bossi; c) Tony Montano

5 In which country did he lose the light-middleweight title in his second defence? a) Japan; b) South Korea; c) Nicaragua

6 Which former British middleweight champion did he outpoint over 10 rounds in Milan in 1965? a) John McCormack; b) Wally Swift; c) Mick Leahy

7 How many fights did he win before suffering his first defeat? a) 52 fights; b) 62 fights; c) 72 fights

8 Which British fighter did he outpoint in his comeback contest after his first defeat? a) Harry Scott; b) Nat Jacobs; c) Les McAteer

How many contests did Nino have during his professional career? a) 80; b) 90; c) 110

 In which year did he have his final fight? a) 1969; b) 1967; c) 1971

 Where was he born? a) Milan; b) Trieste; c) Turin

 From whom did he take the world middleweight title for the first time in 1967? a) Paul Pender; b) Joey Giardello; c) Emile Griffith

 Which former world middleweight champion outpointed him in a non-title fight in New York? a) Dick Tiger; b) Gene Fullmer; c) Terry Downes

 In which round was he knocked out by Carlos Monzon in their first world title fight? a) Eighth round; b) Tenth round; c) Twelfth round

 What was the venue for the final fight of his career, a return against Monzon? a) Monte Carlo; b) Madrid; c) Paris

BIG FIGHT QUIZ No 5 ANSWERS

NIGEL BENN: 1. Army; 2. West Ham; 3. Middle-weight; 4. Burt McCarthy; 5. The Dark Destroyer; 6. Seven rounds; 7. Alexandra Palace; 8. Umaru Sanda; 9. 1964; 10. Ilford; 11. Brian Lynch; 12. Anthony Logan; 13. First round; 14. Glasgow; 15. Frank Maloney.

SCORECARD

Points:

Result:

THE BIG FIGHT QUIZ No. 7

IN THIS CORNER

Jack (Kid) Berg

Award yourself a points win if you get six or more right. It's a draw if you get five right. You win by a knockout if you get 10 or more right.

1 What was Jack (Kid) Berg's name before he became a professional boxer? a) Judah Bergman; b) Jacob Berger; c) Johann Bergski

2 How old was he when he made his professional debut? a) Fourteen; b) Fifteen; c) Sixteen

3 By which nickname was he popularly known? a) Jewel of the East End; b) Cyclone Kid; c) Whitechapel Whirlwind

4 Which future British featherweight champion ended his unbeaten run after 20 fights? a) Johnny Curley; b) Johnny Cuthbert; c) Johnny McGrory

5 How many officially recorded professional fights did he have? a) 172; b) 182; c) 192

6 Who did he beat to become world junior welterweight champion in 1930? a) Billy Petrolle; b) Kid Chocolate; c) Mushy Callahan

7 At which venue did he win the world championship? a) Royal Albert Hall; b) Wembley Stadium; c) Upton Park

8 Who stopped him in three rounds when he challenged for the world lightweight title? a) Barney Ross; b) Tony Canzoneri; c) Lou Ambers

In which year did he make his professional debut?
a) 1924; b) 1928; c) 1920

 Who was his English manager?
a) Jack Solomons; b) Harry Levene; c) Sydney Hulls

 How many years did Jack's remarkable career last?
a) 15 years; b) 17 years; c) 21 years

 Who did he beat for the British lightweight title on his return from America? a) Harry Mizler; b) Al Foreman; c) Jimmy Walsh

 Where did he fight Laurie Stevens for the British Empire title in 1936? a) Melbourne; b) Johannesburg; c) Montreal

 Which British champion did he beat on a second round foul in a non-title fight late in his career? a) Dave Crowley; b) Nel Tarleton; c) Eric Boon

 Who was the outstanding American coach who trained him in the United States? a) Ray Arcel; b) Charley Goldman; c) Whitey Bimstein

BIG FIGHT QUIZ No 6 ANSWERS

NINO BENVENUTI: 1. Rome, 1960; 2. Welterweight; 3. Sixth round; 4. Sandro Mazzinghi; 5. South Korea; 6. Mick Leahy; 7. 72 fights; 8. Harry Scott; 9. 90 fights; 10. 1971; 11. Trieste; 12. Emile Griffith; 13. Dick Tiger; 14. Twelfth round; 15. Monte Carlo.

SCORECARD

Points:

Result:

IN THIS CORNER

Frank Bruno

Award yourself a points win if you get eight or more right. It's a draw if you get seven right. You win by a knockout if you get 12 or more right.

1 Which club was Frank Bruno representing when he won the ABA heavyweight title? a) Hammersmith; b) Sir Philip Game ABC; c) Repton ABC

2 How old was he when he won the ABA championship? a) Eighteen; b) Nineteen; c) Twenty

3 In which South American city did he have an eye operation before getting his professional licence? a) Bogota; b) Montevideo; c) Santiago

4 How many times was he beaten during his 21-bout amateur career? a) Once; b) Twice; c) Three times

5 Where is the Terry Lawless gymnasium at which he prepared for his professional debut? a) Wandsworth; b) Canning Town; c) Shoreditch

6 In which city did he have his first overseas fight against Ali Lukusa? a) Milan; b) Monte Carlo; c) West Berlin

7 Who was the first opponent to take him the distance? a) Phil Brown; b) Jeff Jordan; c) Scott LeDoux

8 In which round did he stop Jumbo Cummings after recovering from a first round fright? a) Fifth round; b) Sixth round; c) Seventh round

How many contests did he win before his first defeat?
a) 19; b) 21; c) 23

 In which year did he make his professional debut?
a) 1980; b) 1981; c) 1982

 Bonecrusher Smith knocked him out in which round?
a) Tenth round; b) Eleventh round; c) Twelfth round

 Who did he knock out in two rounds in a Commonwealth title eliminator? a) Eddie Neilson; b) Winston Allen; c) Ken Lakusta

 In which city did he make his American debut when knocking out Mike Jameson in the second round? a) Washington; b) Chicago; c) New York

In which round did he knock out Anders Eklund when winning the European championship? a) Fourth round; b) Fifth round; c) Sixth round

 Who was the referee for his world championship challenge against Mike Tyson in 1989? a) Richard Steele; b) Carlos Padilla; c) Arthur Mercante

BIG FIGHT QUIZ No 7 ANSWERS

JACK (KID) BERG: 1. Judah Bergman; 2. Fourteen; 3. Whitechapel Whirlwind; 4. Johnny Cuthbert; 5. 192; 6. Mushy Callahan; 7. Royal Albert Hall; 8. Tony Canzoneri; 9..1924; 10. Harry Levene; 11. 21 years; 12. Harry Mizler; 13. Johannesburg; 14. Eric Boon; 15. Ray Arcel.

SCORECARD

Points:

Result:

IN THIS CORNER

Ken Buchanan

Award yourself a points win if you get seven or more right. It's a draw if you get six right. You win by a knockout if you get 11 or more right.

In which Scottish city was Ken Buchanan born and raised?
a) Glasgow; b) Edinburgh; c) Aberdeen

At which weight did he win an ABA championship?
a) Bantamweight; b) Featherweight; c) Lightweight

For part of his career he was managed by which former British champion ? a) Eddie Thomas; b) Terry Downes; c) Cliff Curvis

How many winning fights did he have before his first defeat?
a) 21; b) 25; c) 33

Which European champion inflicted his first defeat?
a) Pedro Carrasco; b) Franco Brondi; c) Miguel Velazquez

In which round did he knock out Maurice Cullen to win the British lightweight championship? a) Sixth round; b) Ninth round; c) Eleventh round

Against whom did he retain the British title in his first defence? a) Brian Hudson; b) Ivan Whiter; c) John McMillan

In which city did he beat Ismael Laguna to become world lightweight champion in 1971? a) San Juan; b) Tijuana; c) Caracas

How many contests did Buchanan have during his career?
a) 50; b) 60; c) 70

In which year did he have his final fight? a) 1979; b) 1981; c) 1983

How many times was he beaten inside the distance?
a) Once; b) Twice; c) Three times

Who took the world lightweight title from him with a victory in the 13th round? a) Mando Ramos; b) Roberto Duran; c) Rodolfo Gonzalez

Which former world champion did he stop in six rounds in the fight after losing his title? a) Carlos Ortiz; b) Joe Brown; c) Flash Elorde

In which city was he beaten by Guts Ishimatsu when bidding to regain the world title? a) Los Angeles; b) Tokyo; c) Barcelona

Who beat him in a European title fight in Copenhagen?
a) Francisco Leon; b) Charlie Nash; c) Joey Gibilisco

SCORECARD

Points:

Result:

| THE BIG FIGHT QUIZ No. 10 |  | **IN THIS CORNER**
 # Joe Bugner
 Award yourself a points win if you get seven or more right. It's a draw if you get six right. You win by a knockout if you get 11 or more right. |

 How old was Joe Bugner when he made his professional debut? a) Seventeen; b) Eighteen; c) Nineteen

 Who was his manager throughout the first phase of his career? a) Terry Lawless; b) Sam Burns; c) Andy Smith

 Before turning professional Joe was oustanding in which athletics event? a) Hammer throw; b) Shot putt; c) Discus throw

 Which opponent knocked him out in the third round in his professional debut? a) Billy Wynter; b) Obe Hepburn; c) Paul Brown

 In which round did he stop former British champion Brian London in 1970? a) Fifth round; b) Seventh round; c) Ninth round

 Who was the referee when he was given a disputed points decision over Henry Cooper? a) Tommy Little; b) Jack Hart; c) Harry Gibbs

 Where did he fight Muhammad Ali the first time they met? a) Las Vegas; b) Atlantic City; c) New York

 To whom did he lose the British title in his first defence in 1971? a) Danny McAlinden; b) Jack Bodell; c) Bunny Johnson

In which country was Joe born?
a) Czechoslovakia; b) Rumania;
c) Hungary

 How old was he when he fought Frank Bruno?
a) 33; b) 35; c) 37

 In which round was he stopped by American Earnie Shavers?
a) Second; b) Fifth; c) Seventh

 Which former world champion did he fight immediately after his first contest with Ali? a) Floyd Patterson; b) George Foreman; c) Joe Frazier

 Who did he knock out in eight rounds to regain the European title? a) Jurgen Blin; b) Jose Urtain; c) Karl Mildenberger

 Which football ground was the venue for his fight against Frank Bruno? a) Highbury Stadium; b) White Hart Lane; c) Loftus Road

 In which round was he stopped by Bruno in the final fight of his career? a) Eighth round; b) Ninth round; c) Tenth round

29

THE BIG FIGHT QUIZ No. 11

IN THIS CORNER

Primo Carnera

Award yourself a points win if you get six or more right. It's a draw if you get five right. You win by a knockout if you get 10 or more right.

 1 What was he working as when persuaded to take up professional boxing? a) Blacksmith; b) Circus strongman; c) Bricklayer

 2 In which country did he have his early professional fights? a) Italy; b) France; c) Germany

 3 Which British champion did he knock out in two rounds in London in 1930? a) Phil Scott; b) Frank Goddard; c) Reggie Meen

 4 By which nickname was he popularly known? a) The Tower of Pisa; b) King Kong; c) The Ambling Alp

 5 Which British-based heavyweight outpointed him in London in 1932? a) Jack Petersen; b) Ben Foord; c) Larry Gains

 6 In which round did he knock out Jack Sharkey to become world heavyweight champion? a) Sixth round; b) Eighth round; c) Tenth round

 7 In which city did he make the first defence of the championship? a) Paris; b) Rome; c) Munich

 8 What was the nationality of Paolino Uzcudun, his opponent in his first title defence? a) French; b) Spanish; c) Italian

How many of his 103 contests did he win inside the distance?
a) 59; b) 69; c) 79

 In which year did he have his final fight? a) 1942; b) 1944; c) 1946

 Where was he born? a) Rimini; b) Sequals; c) Genoa

 Which former world light-heavyweight champion challenged him for the title? a) Tommy Loughran; b) Maxie Rosenbloom; c) Bob Olin

 How many times did Max Baer knock him down before stopping him in the 11th round? a) Seven times; b) Nine times; c) Eleven times

 In which round did Joe Louis stop him in a non-title fight in 1935? a) Fourth round; b) Sixth round; c) Eighth round

 What did he become at the end of his career? a) Professional wrestler; b) American football linebacker; c) Weightlifter

SCORECARD

Points:

Result:

IN THIS CORNER

Georges Carpentier

Award yourself a points win if you get six or more right. It's a draw if you get five right. You win by a knockout if you get 10 or more right.

 How old was Georges Carpentier when he had his first professional contest? a) Thirteen; b) Fourteen; c) Fifteen

 At which weight did he make his debut?
a) Flyweight; b) Bantamweight; c) Featherweight

 By which nickname was he popularly known? a) The Orchid Man; b) The Pride of Paris; c) The Gay Executioner

 Which British champion did he stop in 10 rounds to win the European welterweight title in 1911? a) Joe White; b) Curley Watson; c) Young Joseph

 In which round did he knock out Bombardier Billy Wells in their first fight in 1913? a) Second round; b) Fourth round; c) Sixth round

 Who did he knock out in eight rounds in defence of his European heavyweight title in 1919? a) Frank Goddard; b) Dick Smith; c) Pat O'Keefe

 Where did he beat Battling Levinsky to win the world light-heavyweight title? a) Baltimore; b) Jersey City; c) San Francisco

 Against which champion did he make an unsuccessful bid for the world heavyweight title? a) Jess Willard; b) Max Schmeling; c) Jack Dempsey

32

In which year did he make his final ring appearance?
a) 1927; b) 1929; c) 1931

 How many official professional contests did he have?
a) 109; b) 119; c) 129

 How many defeats did he suffer during his career?
a) Nine; b) Fourteen; c) Seventeen

 Which future world heavyweight champion stopped him in a non-title fight in 1924? a) Jack Sharkey; b) James J. Braddock; c) Gene Tunney

 Who took the world light-heavyweight title from him with a sixth round stoppage? a) Battling Siki; b) Mike McTigue; c) Jack Delaney

 In which round did he knock out Ted 'Kid' Lewis in their controversial world title fight in 1922? a) First round; b) Second round; c) Third

 Which British heavyweight champion did he twice knock out in one round? a) James Moir; b) Iron Hague; c) Joe Beckett

SCORECARD

Points:

Result:

IN THIS CORNER

Ezzard Charles

Award yourself a points win if you get six or more right. It's a draw if you get five right. You win by a knockout if you get 10 or more right.

 At which weight was Charles Golden Gloves champion before turning professional? a) Middleweight; b) Light-heavyweight; c) Heavyweight

 By which ring nickname was he popularly known?
a) The Cincinnati Cobra; b) The Black Flash; c) The Human Cyclone

 Which of these world light-heavyweight champions did he beat three times in non-title fights? a) Harold Johnson; b) Archie Moore; c) Billy Conn

 Which of these world light-heavyweight champions did he outpoint five times? a) Gus Lesnevich; b) Willie Pastrano; c) Joey Maxim

 Who did he beat for the undisputed world heavyweight championship in 1950? a) Joe Louis; b) Lee Oma; c) Tami Mauriello

 In which round did Jersey Joe Walcott knock him out in their 1951 world title fight? a) Seventh round; b) Ninth round; c) Eleventh round

 How many times did he and Jersey Joe Walcott meet in heavyweight title fights? a) Three times; b) Four times; c) Five times

 Who outpointed him twice over 10 rounds inside a month in 1954? a) Tommy Jackson; b) Harry Matthews; c) Roland LaStarza

34

How many contests did he have during his professional career?
a) 112; b) 122; c) 132

 In which US state was he born?
a) Alabama; b) Mississippi;
c) Georgia

 In which year did he make his final ring appearance?
a) 1956; b) 1959; c) 1961

 Which contender did he stop in two rounds to clinch a world title shot against Rocky Marciano? a) Nino Valdes; b) Rex Layne; c) Bob Satterfield

 In which city did both his world title contests against Rocky Marciano take place? a) New York; b) Los Angeles; c) Las Vegas

 In which round did Marciano knock him out in their second world championship contest? a) Sixth round; b) Eighth round; c) Tenth round

 Against which British boxer was he disqualified in his only fighting visit to London? a) Brian London; b) Don Cockell; c) Dick Richardson

SCORECARD

Points:

Result:

IN THIS CORNER

Dave Charnley

Award yourself a points win if you get seven or more right. It's a draw if you get six right. You win by a knockout if you get 11 or more right.

 At which weight was Dave Charnley an ABA champion before turning professional? a) Bantamweight; b) Featherweight; c) Lightweight

 In which district was he born and raised? a) Hungerford; b) Bedford; c) Dartford

 Who was his manager throughout his professional career? a) Benny Jacobs; b) George Middleton; c) Arthur Boggis

 How old was he when he captured the British lightweight championship? a) Nineteen; b) Twenty-one; c) Twenty-five

 From whom did he take the British title? a) Joe Lucy; b) Sammy McCarthy; c) Tommy McGovern

 Which opponent gave him his first defeat when he challenged for the Commonwealth title? a) Johnny van Rensburg; b) Pat Ford; c) Willie Toweel

 In which round did he win by a knockout in the return fight for the Commonwealth title? a) Sixth round; b) Eighth round; c) Tenth round

 In which country did he lose the Commonwealth title to Bunny Grant? a) Jamaica; b) Canada; c) Australia

In which year did he make his professional debut?
a) 1954; b) 1956; c) 1958

 How many contests did he have during his professional career?
a) 41; b) 51; c) 61

 In which year did he make his final ring appearance?
a) 1963; b) 1965; c) 1967

 In which round did he retire with a cut eye when making his first bid for the world title against Joe Brown? a) First round; b) Fifth round; c) Ninth round

 Where was his third non-title fight with Joe Brown staged in which he avenged two previous defeats? a) Manchester; b) Nottingham; c) Liverpool

 Who did he beat in a British title fight to win a Lonsdale Belt outright? a) Vic Andretti; b) Dave Coventry; c) Maurice Cullen

 How quickly did he knock out Darkie Hughes in a British title defence? a) 30 seconds; b) 40 seconds; c) 50 seconds

BIG FIGHT QUIZ No 13 ANSWERS

EZZARD CHARLES: 1. Middleweight; 2. The Cincinnati Cobra; 3. Archie Moore; 4. Joey Maxim; 5. Joe Louis; 6. Seventh; 7. Four times; 8. Tommy Jackson; 9. 122; 10. Georgia; 11. 1959; 12. Bob Satterfield; 13. New York; 14. Eighth; 15. Dick Richardson.

SCORECARD

Points:

Result:

IN THIS CORNER

Don Cockell

Award yourself a points win if you get seven or more right. It's a draw if you get six right. You win by a knockout if you get 11 or more right.

In which area of London was Don Cockell based when he first started his boxing career? a) Bermondsey; b) Blackfriars; c) Battersea

What was his job before he became a full-time professional boxer? a) Bus driver; b) Electrician; c) Blacksmith

Who was his manager when he challenged for the world heavyweight title? a) John Simpson; b) George Dingley; c) Benny Huntman

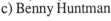
Who did he beat for the vacant British light-heavyweight championship in 1950? a) Dennis Powell; b) George Walker; c) Mark Hart

In which round did he knock out Albert Finch in defence of the light-heavyweight championship? a) Seventh; b) Ninth; c) Eleventh

Who took the light-heavyweight title from him with an 11th round stoppage in 1952? a) Alex Buxton; b) Randolph Turpin; c) Ron Barton

He outpointed which champion to win the British heavyweight title in 1953? a) Johnny Williams; b) Jack Gardner; c) Jack London

Which top-ranking American did he twice outpoint to earn himself a world title shot? a) Joe Baksi; b) Harry Matthews; c) Lee Oma

In which year did he make his professional debut?
a) 1946; b) 1948; c) 1950

 How many fights did he have during his career?
a) 59; b) 69; c) 79

 In which year did Cockell have the final fight of his eventful career before hanging up his gloves?
a) 1956; b) 1958; c) 1960

 Where was his world heavyweight championship contest against Rocky Marciano staged? a) San Francisco; b) Los Angeles; c) Miami

 In which round was he stopped when challenging Marciano for the world championship? a) Second round; b) Sixth round; c) Ninth round

 Where did he successfully defend the Commonwealth heavyweight title against Johnny Arthur? a) Vancouver; b) Johannesburg; c) Sydney

 He retired after being beaten in two rounds by which opponent? a) Kitione Lave; b) Nino Valdes; c) Roland La Starza

BIG FIGHT QUIZ No 14 ANSWERS

DAVE CHARNLEY: 1. Featherweight; 2. Dartford; 3. Arthur Boggis; 4. Twenty-one; 5. Joe Lucy; 6. Willie Toweel; 7. Tenth round; 8. Jamaica; 9. 1954; 10. 61 contests; 11. 1965; 12. Fifth round; 13. Manchester; 14. Maurice Cullen; 15. 40 seconds.

SCORECARD

Points:

Result:

THE BIG FIGHT QUIZ No. 16

IN THIS CORNER
John Conteh

Award yourself a points win if you get eight or more right. It's a draw if you get seven right. You win by a knockout if you get 12 or more right.

1 At which weight did John Conteh win a Commonwealth Games gold medal? a) Welterweight; b) Light-middleweight; c) Middleweight

2 In which district was he born and raised?
a) Merseyside; b) Old Trafford; b) South Shields

3 Who was the only fighter to beat him before he became world champion? a) Bill Drover; b) Dave Matthews; c) Eddie Duncan

4 In which round did he stop Rudi Schmidtke to win the European light-heavyweight title? a) Tenth round; b) Twelfth round; c) Fourteenth round

5 Who did he outpoint to add the British and Commonwealth titles to his European championship? a) Chris Finnegan; b) Billy Aird; c) Eddie Avoth

6 What nationality was Tom Bogs, who he stopped in six rounds in a European title defence? a) French; b) Dutch; c) Danish

7 In which round did he stop Chris Finnegan in their second championship contest? a) Fourth round; b) Sixth round; c) Eighth round

8 Who did he beat to win the vacant WBC world light-heavyweight title? a) Victor Galindez; b) Jesse Burnett; c) Jorge Ahumada

In which year did he make his professional debut?
a) 1969; b) 1971; c) 1973

 How many professional fights did he have?
a) 39; b) 49; c) 59

 In which year did he make his final ring appearance before hanging up his gloves?
a) 1978; b) 1979; c) 1980

 Who did he stop in five rounds in his first defence of the world title? a) Lonnie Bennett; b) Willie Taylor; c) Lennie Hutchins

 In which country did he successfully defend the world title against Alvaro Lopez? a) Holland; b) Sweden; c) Denmark

 Who outpointed him in a world title contest in Belgrade?
a) Miguel Angel Cuello; b) Mate Parlov; c) Marvin Johnson

 In which round was he stopped by Matthew Saad Muhammad in their second world title fight? a) Second round; b) Fourth round; c) Sixth round

SCORECARD

Points:

Result:

THE BIG FIGHT QUIZ No. 17		IN THIS CORNER

Henry Cooper

Award yourself a points win if you get eight or more right. It's a draw if you get seven right. You win by a knockout if you get 12 or more right.

 In which branch of the armed forces was he serving when he was ABA light-heavyweight champion? a) Army; b) Royal Navy; c) Royal Air Force

 What was his job before he became a full-time professional boxer? a) Roof tiler; b) Plasterer; c) Plumber

 Who did he knock out in seven rounds in a return fight to avenge his first defeat as a pro? a) Peter Bates; b) Hugh Ferns; c) Uber Bacilieri

 How many times did he and Joe Erskine meet, including their three amateur contests? a) Six times; b) Seven times; c) Eight times

 Who did he beat to become British heavyweight champion for the first time? a) Brian London; b) Joe Erskine; c) Dick Richardson

 In which round did Ingemar Johansson knock him out in a European title fight in 1957? a) Third round; b) Fifth round; c) Seventh round

 Where did he beat Gawie de Klerk in five rounds in defence of his Commonwealth title? a) Porthcawl; b) Blackpool; c) Nottingham

 Who was the referee when Henry met the then Cassius Clay in 1963? a) Ike Powell; b) George Smith; c) Tommy Little

42

Who managed him throughout his career? a) Jack Burns; b) Arthur Boggis; c) Jim Wicks

 In which year did he make his professional debut? a) 1952; b) 1954; c) 1956

 How many professional fights did he have? a) 45; b) 55; c) 65

 In which round did he knock down Clay in their first meeting? a) Third round; b) Fourth round; c) Sixth round

 At which football ground was his world title fight against Muhammad Ali staged? a) White Hart Lane; b) Stamford Bridge; c) Highbury Stadium

 Which former world champion knocked him out in four rounds in 1966? a) Sonny Liston; b) Joe Frazier; c) Floyd Patterson

 Where did he knock out Piero Tomasoni in a European title fight in 1969? a) Rome; b) Milan; c) Turin

SCORECARD

Points:

Result:

IN THIS CORNER

James J. Corbett

Award yourself a points win if you get six or more right. It's a draw if you get five right. You win by a knockout if you get 10 or more right.

 Where in the United States was James J. Corbett born?
a) Miami; b) San Francisco; c) Seattle

 What was his job outside the ring when he first turned professional? a) Bank clerk; b) Train driver; c) Policeman

 With which famous sporting club did he first make a name for himself as an all-round sportsman? a) Pegasus; b) Olympic; c) Hercules

 What was he nicknamed because of his stylish dress?
a) Dandy Jim; b) Beau Jim; c) Gentleman Jim

 The initial 'J' in James J. Corbett stood for which name?
a) Jack; b) John; c) Jeffrey

 What was the venue for his second fight with Joe Choynski?
a) A barn; b) A stable; c) A barge

 Who portrayed him in the film based on his life story?
a) Ward Bond; b) James Cagney; c) Errol Flynn

 How many rounds did he and Peter Jackson battle with each other before the referee declared a draw ? a) Forty-one; b) Fifty-one; c) Sixty-one

44

How old was he when he won the world title?
a) 22; b) 24; c) 26

 In which year did he become world champion?
a)1892; b) 1896; c) 1900

 How many recorded professionals fights did he have?
a) 19; b) 29; c) 39

 From whom did he win the world title in the first gloved championship? a) Jem Mace; b) Paddy Ryan; c) John L. Sullivan

 In which round did he knock out Englishman Charley Mitchell in his first title defence? a) Third round; b) Twentieth round; c) Thirtieth round

 Against which opponent was he disqualified in the ninth round? a) Tom Sharkey; b) Jake Kilrain; c) Jim McVey

 Who was the champion who stopped him in 10 rounds in his last fight? a) Marvin Hart; b) Tommy Burns; c) James J. Jeffries

SCORECARD

Points:

Result:

45

THE BIG FIGHT QUIZ No. 19

IN THIS CORNER

Brian Curvis

Award yourself a points win if you get seven or more right. It's a draw if you get six right. You win by a knockout if you get 11 or more right.

1 Where was Brian Curvis born and raised as a member of a fighting family? a) Cardiff; b) Newport; c) Swansea

2 To what surname did Brian answer before he became a professional boxer? a) Nancurvis; b) Thomacurvis; c) Joncurvis

3 What relation was his manager, Cliff Curvis? a) Father; b) Brother; c) Uncle

4 At which weight did he win an ABA championship? a) Lightweight; b) Light-welterweight; c) Welterweight

5 How many professional contests had he had before winning the Commonwealth welterweight championship? a) Thirteen; b) Eighteen; c) Twenty-one

6 From which opponent did he take the Commonwealth title? a) George Barnes; b) Johnny van Rensburg; c) Gerald Dreyer

7 Who did he twice outpoint in his first two British championship fights? a) Tommy Molloy; b) Peter Waterman; c) Wally Swift

8 In which round did he knock out Mick Leahy to win his first Lonsdale Belt outright? a) Sixth round; b) Eighth round; c) Tenth round

In which year did he make his professional debut?
a) 1957; b) 1959; c) 1961

 How many contests did he have during his professional career?
a) 37; b) 47; c) 57

 In which year did he make his final ring appearance?
a) 1963; b) 1964; c) 1965

 Who did he force to retire in five rounds to win his second Lonsdale Belt outright? a) Tony Mancini; b) Tony Smith; c) Johnny Cooke

 Where did he challenge Emile Griffith for the world welterweight title? a) New York; b) Porthcawl; c) Wembley

 How was he beaten by Griffith? a) On points; b) Knocked out in the seventh round; c) Stopped with a cut eye

Against whom did he make a final defence before retiring as unbeaten British champion? a) Ralph Charles; b) Shaun Doyle; c) Sammy McSpadden

BIG FIGHT QUIZ No 18 ANSWERS

JAMES J. CORBETT: 1. San Francisco; 2. Bank clerk; 3. Olympic; 4. Gentleman Jim; 5. John; 6. A barge; 7. Errol Flynn; 8. Sixty-one rounds; 9. 26 years old; 10. 1892; 11. 19 fights; 12. John L. Sullivan; 13. Third round; 14. Tom Sharkey; 15. James J. Jeffries.

SCORECARD

Points:

Result:

47

THE BIG FIGHT QUIZ No. 20

IN THIS CORNER

Jack Dempsey

Award yourself a points win if you get seven or more right. It's a draw if you get six right. You win by a knockout if you get 11 or more right.

 1 What was his name before adopting the ring name of Jack ? a) John Henry; b) William Harrison; c) Joseph Patrick

 2 Who managed him throughout the peak years of his career? a) Tex Rickard; b) Joe Jacobs; c) Jack Kearns

 3 By which nickname was he popularly known? a) The Manassa Mauler; b) The Colorado Killer; c) The Fighting Machine

 4 How many times did he have Jess Willard down in the first round when he won the world title? a) Five times; b) Six times; c) Seven times

 5 In which round did he knock out Luis Angel Firpo in their explosive title fight? a) First round; b) Second round; c) Third round

 6 Who was his opponent in the first fight to draw a million dollar gate? a) Georges Carpentier; b) Gene Tunney; c) Billy Miske

 7 Apart from Gene Tunney, who was the only opponent to take him the distance in a title fight? a) Tommy Gibbons; b) Bill Brennan; c) Tom Heeney

 8 He and Gene Tunney met over a total of how many rounds in their two contests? a) Twenty rounds; b) Twenty-five rounds; c) Thirty rounds

In which year did he make his professional debut?
a) 1914; b) 1918; c) 1922

 How many official fights did he have during his career?
a) 79; b) 89; c) 99

 In which year did he have his final fight?
a) 1927; b) 1932; c) 1936

 Where was his world heavyweight championship contest against Jess Willard staged? a) Philadelphia; b) Memphis; c) Toledo

 Which future world champion did he knock out between the two contests with Tunney? a) Max Schmeling; b) James J. Braddock; c) Jack Sharkey

Following his retirement what did he run in New York that became a famous landmark? a) A pub; b) A gymnasium; c) A restaurant

In which round did he knock down Tunney in the 'Battle of the Long Count'? a) Fifth round; b) Seventh round; c) Ninth round

 Following his retirement what did he run in New York that became a famous landmark? a) A pub; b) A gymnasium; c) A restaurant

SCORECARD

Points:

Result:

THE BIG FIGHT QUIZ No. 21

IN THIS CORNER

Terry Downes

Award yourself a points win if you get seven or more right. It's a draw if you get six right. You win by a knockout if you get 11 or more right.

In which district of London was Terry Downes born?
a) Hampstead; b) Tottenham; c) Paddington

In which branch of the United States armed forces did he serve? a) Air Force; b) Army; b) Marines

Which future world champion beat him in his third professional contest? a) Dick Tiger; b) Joey Giardello; c) Emile Griffith

Who did he beat for the vacant British middleweight championship? a) Freddie Cross; b) Phil Edwards; c) Les Allen

In which round did he get stopped by world title contender Spider Webb? a) Fourth round; b) Sixth round; c) Eighth round

How did he lose the British middleweight title to John McCormack? a) On points; b) A cut eye stoppage; c) On a disqualification

In which round did he stop John McCormack in their return title fight? a) Eighth round; b) Tenth round; c) Twelfth round

Where did he make his first challenge for the world middleweight title against Paul Pender? a) Boston; b) Cleveland; c) Milwaukee

In which year did he make his professional debut?
a) 1955; b) 1957; c) 1959

 How many professional fights did he have?
a) 34; b) 44; c) 54

 In which year did he make his final ring appearance?
a) 1964; b) 1966; c) 1968

 At the end of which round did Paul Pender retire in their second world title fight? a) Fifth round; b) Seventh round; c) Ninth round

 Which former world champion did he outpoint after losing the world title back to Pender? a) Ray Robinson; b) Gene Fullmer; c) Carmen Basilio

 Where did he make a bid for the world light-heavyweight title the final contest of his career? a) Birmingham; b) Newcastle; c) Manchester

 Who stopped him in 11 rounds when he challenged for the world light-heavyweight title? a) Eddie Cotton; b) Jose Torres; c) Willie Pastrano

SCORECARD

Points:

Result:

THE BIG FIGHT QUIZ No. 22

IN THIS CORNER
Roberto Duran

Award yourself a points win if you get seven or more right. It's a draw if you get six right. You win by a knockout if you get 11 or more right.

1 In which country was he born and raised?
a) Argentina; b) Uruguay; c) Panama

2 How old was he when he made his professional debut?
a) Sixteen; b) Eighteen; c) Twenty

3 By what nickname is he popularly known? a) Hands of Iron;
b) Hands of Stone; c) Hands of Gold

4 Who was the only man to beat him in his first 74 contests?
a) Lloyd Marshall; b) Hector Thompson; c) Esteban DeJesus

5 In which round did he stop Ken Buchanan to win the world lightweight championship? a) Ninth round; b) Eleventh round; c) Thirteenth round

6 How many times did he successfully defend the lightweight title before relinquishing it? a) Twelve times; b) Fourteen times; c) Sixteen times

7 Who was the only challenger to take him the distance in all his lightweight title defences? a) Ray Lampkin; b) Edwin Viruet; c) Alvaro Rojas

8 Where did he beat Sugar Ray Leonard for the world welterweight title? a) Montreal; b) San José; c) Mexico City

In which year did he make his professional debut?
a) 1963; b) 1965; c) 1967

 He retired during which round in the return with Leonard?
a) 8th; b) 9th; c) 10th

 In which year was he ko'd by Thomas Hearns?
a) 1980; b) 1982; c) 1984

 Which British boxer outpointed him in a non-title fight in America in 1982? a) Jimmy Batten; b) Kirkland Laing; c) Maurice Hope

 Where did he challenge Wilfred Benitez for the world light-middleweight title? a) Mexico City; b) Buenos Aires; c) Las Vegas

 In which round did he stop Davey Moore to win the WBA world light-middleweight title? a) Eighth round; b) Tenth round; c) Twelfth round

 Who did he outpoint to become world middleweight champion in 1989? a) John Mugabi; b) Doug DeWitt; c) Iran Barkley

SCORECARD

Points:

Result:

IN THIS CORNER

Tommy Farr

Award yourself a points win if you get six or more right. It's a draw if you get five right. You win by a knockout if you get 10 or more right.

 How old was he when he started boxing professionally in the fair booths? a) Thirteen; b) Fourteen; c) Fifteen

 In which district of Wales was he born and raised? a) Camarthen; b) Llanelli; c) Tonypandy

 What did he do for a living before becoming a full-time professional boxer? a) Farm labourer; b) Coal miner; c) Lorry driver

 Who outpointed him when he challenged for the British light-heavyweight title? a) Jock McAvoy; b) Len Harvey; c) Eddie Phillips

 He outpointed which champion to capture the British heavyweight title in 1937? a) Ben Foord; b) Jack Petersen; c) Jack London

 Which former world champion did he outpoint at Harringay to clinch a world title shot? a) James J. Braddock; b) Jack Sharkey; c) Max Baer

 In which round did he knock out German heavyweight Walter Neusel? a) First round; b) Second round; c) Third round

 Where did he challenge Joe Louis for the world heavyweight championship? a) Detroit; b) New York; c) Chicago

54

In which year did he make his professional debut?
a) 1926; b) 1928; c) 1930

 How many recorded fights did he have during his career?
a) 97; b) 107; c) 127

 In which year did he make his last ring appearance?
a) 1948; b) 1950; c) 1953

 How old was he when he made a post-war comeback to the ring? a) Thirty-four; b) Thirty-six; c) Thirty-eight

 How many fights did he have in his comeback spell?
a) Eleven; b) Fifteen; c) Nineteen

 Who stopped him in seven rounds in the final contest of his career? a) Johnny Williams; b) Jack Gardner; c) Don Cockell

 What job did he turn to with success in his retirement?
a) Sports journalism; b) Dairy farming; c) Motor mechanic

BIG FIGHT QUIZ No 22 ANSWERS

ROBERTO DURAN: 1. Panama; 2. Sixteen; 3. Hands of Stone; 4. Esteban DeJesus; 5. Thirteenth round; 6. Twelve times; 7. Edwin Viruet; 8. Montreal; 9. 1967; 10. Eighth round; 11. 1984; 12. Kirkland Laing; 13. Las Vegas; 14. Eighth round; 15. Iran Barkley

SCORECARD

Points:

Result:

THE BIG FIGHT QUIZ No. 24

IN THIS CORNER

Chris Finnegan

Award yourself a points win if you get seven or more right. It's a draw if you get six right. You win by a knockout if you get 11 or more right.

1 At which Olympics did Chris Finnegan win a gold medal?
a) Tokyo 1964; b) Mexico 1968; c) Munich 1972

2 At what weight was he the Olympic champion?
a) Light-middleweight; b) Middleweight; c) Light-heavy-weight

3 Who managed him throughout his career?
a) Jim Wicks; b) Bobby Neill; c) Sam Burns

4 From whom did he take the British and Commonwealth light-heavyweight title in 1971? a) Eddie Avoth; b) Young McCormack; c) Roy John

5 Where did he challenge Conny Velensek for the European light-heavyweight title in 1971? a) Copenhagen; b) Barcelona; c) Berlin

6 How did Velensek retain the European title in their first contest? a) On a disqualification; b) On a draw; c) On a cut-eye stoppage

7 Who did Chris knock out in eight rounds in his first defence of the European title? a) Jan Lubbers; b) Tom Bogs; c) Piero del Papa

8 In which round was he ko'd when fighting Bob Foster for the world light-heavyweight title? a) Tenth round; b) Twelfth round; c) Fourteenth round

In which year did he make his professional debut?
a) 1968; b) 1969; c) 1970

 How many contests did he have during his professional career?
a) 47; b) 57; c) 67

 In which year did he make his final ring appearance?
a) 1972; b) 1974; c) 1976

 What was the venue for both his title fights against John Conteh? a) Royal Albert Hall; b) Wembley Arena; c) Earls Court

 To whom did he lose the European title six weeks after his world title defeat? a) Rudiger Schmitdke; b) Domenico Adinolfi; c) Mate Parlov

 Who did he beat to win the British light-heavyweight title for a second time? a) Tim Wood; b) Bunny Johnson; c) Johnny Frankham

 At which weight was his brother, Kevin, a champion of Europe? a) Light-middleweight; b) Middleweight; c) Light-heavyweight

SCORECARD

Points:

Result:

IN THIS CORNER

Bob Fitzsimmons

Award yourself a points win if you get six or more right. It's a draw if you get five right. You win by a knockout if you get 10 or more right.

In which English county was he born?
a) Devonshire; b) Somerset; c) Cornwall

Where did make his official debut as a professional boxer?
a) Wellington, New Zealand; b) Sydney, Australia;
c) Vancouver, Canada

What was his job before he concentrated full time on professional boxing? a) Sheep farmer; b) Bank clerk; c) Blacksmith

From whom did he take the world middleweight championship in 1891? a) Kid McCoy; b) Stanley Ketchel; c) 'Nonpareil' Jack Dempsey

Where did he challenge James J. Corbett for the world heavyweight championship? a) Reno; b) Carson City; c) Coney Island

In which round did he knock out Corbett with his famous solar plexus punch? a) Tenth round; b) Twelfth round; c) Fourteenth round

Who took the world heavyweight title from him with an 11th round knockout in 1899? a) James J. Jeffries; b) Marvin Hart; c) Tommy Burns

In which round was he knocked out by James J. Jeffries when bidding to regain the title? a) Eighth round; b) Twelfth round; c) Twentieth round

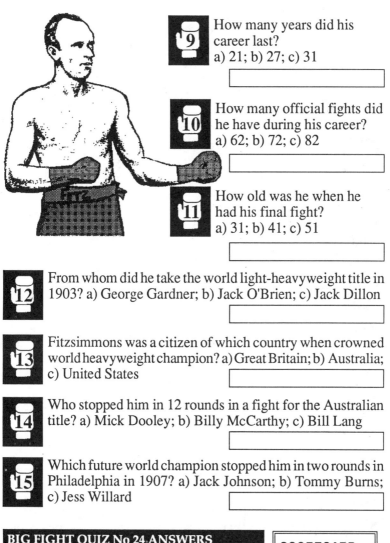

9 How many years did his career last?
a) 21; b) 27; c) 31

10 How many official fights did he have during his career?
a) 62; b) 72; c) 82

11 How old was he when he had his final fight?
a) 31; b) 41; c) 51

12 From whom did he take the world light-heavyweight title in 1903? a) George Gardner; b) Jack O'Brien; c) Jack Dillon

13 Fitzsimmons was a citizen of which country when crowned world heavyweight champion? a) Great Britain; b) Australia; c) United States

14 Who stopped him in 12 rounds in a fight for the Australian title? a) Mick Dooley; b) Billy McCarthy; c) Bill Lang

15 Which future world champion stopped him in two rounds in Philadelphia in 1907? a) Jack Johnson; b) Tommy Burns; c) Jess Willard

BIG FIGHT QUIZ No 24 ANSWERS

CHRIS FINNEGAN: 1. Mexico 1968; 2. Middle-weight; 3. Sam Burns; 4. Eddie Avoth; 5. Berlin; 6. On a draw; 7. Jan Lubbers; 8. Fourteenth; 9. 1968; 10. 47 contests; 11. 1976; 12. Wembley Arena; 13. Rudiger Schmitdke; 14. Johnny Frankham; 15. Middleweight.

SCORECARD

Points:

Result:

59

THE BIG FIGHT QUIZ No. 26

IN THIS CORNER

George Foreman

Award yourself a points win if you get eight or more right. It's a draw if you get seven right. You win by a knockout if you get 12 or more right.

 At which Olympics was George Foreman the gold medallist in the heavyweight division? a) Tokyo 1964; b) Mexico 1968; c) Munich 1972

 In which state in America was he born and raised? a) Michigan; b) California; c) Texas

 How many successive victories did he notch up before his first defeat? a) 30; b) 35; c) 40

 Which future world title contender did he stop in three rounds in his fourth contest? a) George Chuvalo; b) Chuck Wepner; c) Oscar Bonavena

 Where did he challenge Joe Frazier for the world heavyweight championship? a) Guyana; b) Jamaica; c) Trinidad

 How many times did he knock Frazier down before the referee stopped their first fight? a) Four times; b) Five times; c) Six times

 In which round did he stop Frazier in their second non-title fight? a) Fifth round; b) Seventh round; c) Ninth round

 Where did he defend his title against José King Roman? a) Tokyo; b) Seoul; c) Honolulu

In which year did he make his professional debut?
a) 1965; b) 1967; c) 1969

 How many fights did he have before his first retirement?
a) 37; b) 47; c) 57

 In which round did he stop Ken Norton?
a) Second; b) Third; c) Fourth

 Where did Muhammad Ali challenge him for the title in their 'Rumble in the Jungle'? a) Nigeria; b) Uganda; c) Zaire

 In which round did Ali knock him out in their title contest?
a) Sixth round; b) Seventh round; c) Eighth round

 Who outpointed him over 12 rounds to force his decision to retire in 1977? a) Ron Lyle; b) Charley Polite; c) Jimmy Young

15 How old was he when he started his comeback campaign?
a) 37; b) 39; c) 41

BIG FIGHT QUIZ No 25 ANSWERS

BOB FITZSIMMONS: 1. Cornwall; 2. Sydney; 3. Blacksmith; 4. Jack Dempsey; 5. Carson City; 6. Fourteenth round; 7. James J. Jeffries; 8. Eighth round; 9. 31 years; 10. 62 contests; 11. 51 years old; 12. George Gardner; 13. United States; 14. Bill Lang; 15. Jack Johnson.

SCORECARD

Points:

Result:

IN THIS CORNER

Joe Frazier

Award yourself a points win if you get eight or more right. It's a draw if you get seven right. You win by a knockout if you get 12 or more right.

1 In which state in America was he born?
a) South Carolina; b) Tennessee; c) Alabama

2 At which Olympics did he win the gold medal in the heavyweight division? a) Melbourne 1956; b) Rome 1960; c) Tokyo 1964

3 By what nickname was he popularly known?
a) Scorchin' Joe; b) Joltin' Joe; c) Smokin' Joe

4 How many fights did he win in succession before his first defeat? a) 29 contests; b) 39 contests; c) 49 contests

5 Which of his old amateur rivals did he beat to win the New York version of the world title? a) Doug Jones; b) Tony Doyle; c) Buster Mathis

6 At the end of which round did he force Jimmy Ellis to retire in their fight for the undisputed title? a) Fourth round; b) Sixth round; c) Eighth round

7 Which world light-heavyweight champion challenged him for the heavyweight crown? a) Victor Galindez; b) Jose Torres; c) Bob Foster

8 Where did he outpoint Muhammad Ali in the first of their three meetings? a) Las Vegas; b) New York; c) Philadelphia

62

In which year did he make his professional debut?
a) 1963; b) 1965; c) 1967

Who was his manager?
a) Yancy Durham; b) Cus D'Amato; c) Al Weill

In which round did he stop Jerry Quarry?
a) 5th; b) 7th; c) 9th

Where was his third fight against Muhammad Ali staged?
a) Manila; b) Munich; c) Marbella

After how many rounds did he retire against Ali in their second title fight? a) Tenth round; b) Twelfth round; c) Fourteenth round

Against whom did he have a return contest in a non-title fight in Melbourne in 1975? a) Oscar Bonavena; b) Jimmy Ellis; c) George Foreman

Who held him to a draw over twelve rounds in the final fight of his career? a) Floyd 'Jumbo' Cummings; b) Ron Stander; c) Terry Daniels

SCORECARD

Points:

Result:

IN THIS CORNER

Herol Graham

Award yourself a points win if you get eight or more right. It's a draw if you get seven right. You win by a knockout if you get 12 or more right.

 In which English city was he born?
a) Sheffield; b) Nottingham; c) Birmingham

 Who has trained him throughout his peak years as a professional, apart from a short break? a) Bernard Ingle; b) Bobby Neill; c) Freddie Hill

 How many fights did he have before winning the British light-middleweight title? a) Sixteen; b) Twenty; c) Twenty-six

 From whom did he take the British light-middleweight championship? a) Jimmy Batten; b) Prince Rodney; c) Pat Thomas

 From whom did he take the Commonwealth light-middleweight championship? a) Kenny Bristol; b) Clyde Gray; c) Al Korovou

 In which round did he stop Chris Christian in his first defence of the Commonwealth title? a) Seventh round; b) Ninth round; c) Twelfth round

 Where did he successfully defend his Commonwealth title against Hunter Clay? a) Kampala; b) Lusaka; c) Lagos

 In which round did he knock out Clemente Tshinza to win the European light-middleweight title? a) Second round; b) Fourth round; c) Sixth round

In which year did he make his professional debut?
a) 1978; b) 1980; c) 1982

 He won his first European title after how many fights?
a) 20; b) 24; c) 28

 Who took over as his manager? a) Frank Warren; b) Barney Eastwood; c) Barry Hearn

 Who did he knock out in one round to win the vacant British middleweight title? a) Jimmy Price; b) Eddie Burke; c) Roy Gumbs

 In which round did he stop Ayub Kalule to win the European middleweight championship? a) Tenth round; b) Twelfth round; c) Fourteenth round

 Where did he make a successful defence of his European title against Mark Kaylor? a) The Crucible, Sheffield; b) Royal Albert Hall; c) Wembley

Who was the first opponent to beat him as a professional?
a) Hugo Corro; b) Milton McCrory; c) Sumbu Kalambay

IN THIS CORNER

Rocky Graziano

Award yourself a points win if you get six or more right. It's a draw if you get five right. You win by a knockout if you get 10 or more right.

1 What was Rocky Graziano's real name?
a) Rocco Barbella; b) Rocco Luciano; c) Rocco Barbota

2 What was the title of his autobiography?
a) The Harder They Fall; b) For Whom the Bell Tolls; c) Somebody Up There Likes Me

3 Which Hollywood star portrayed him in the film of the book? a) Marlon Brando; b) Rod Steiger; c) Paul Newman

4 In which city was he born and raised? a) Washington DC; b) Milwaukee; c) New York City

5 At which weight was he a Golden Gloves champion before turning professional? a) Welterweight; b) Middleweight; c) Light-heavyweight

6 Which former world champion did he stop in two rounds to set up a world title shot? a) Billy Soose; b) Marty Servo; c) Ken Overlin

7 How many times did he meet Tony Zale for the world middleweight championship? a) Twice; b) Three times; c) Four times

8 In which round did Zale knock out Graziano in their first title fight? a) Third round; b) Sixth round; c) Ninth round

In which year did he make his professional debut?
a) 1938; b) 1942; c) 1944

 How many contests did he have during his professional career?
a) 63; b) 73; c) 83

 In which year did he make his final ring appearance?
a) 1948; b) 1952; c) 1956

 Where did he take the title from Tony Zale with a sixth round knockout victory? a) Pittsburgh; b) Jersey City; c) Chicago

 In which round was he knocked out by Zale in their third title fight? a) Third round; b) Fourth round; c) Fifth round

 Who knocked him out when he made a final challenge for the world middleweight title? a) Marcel Cerdan; b) Ray Robinson; c) Bobo Olson

 What did he become at the end of his eventful career?
a) A nightclub comedian; b) A singer; c) An actor

SCORECARD

Points:

Result:

THE BIG FIGHT QUIZ No. 30

IN THIS CORNER

Emile Griffith

Award yourself a points win if you get seven or more right. It's a draw if you get six right. You win by a knockout if you get 11 or more right.

1 Where was Emile Griffith born and raised?
a) Solomon Islands; b) Leeward Islands; c) Virgin Islands

2 Who was his manager in the peak years of his career?
a) Johnny Buckley; b) Pat Petronelli; c) Gil Clancy

3 In which round did he stop Benny Paret in their tragic third world welterweight title fight? a) Eighth round; b) Tenth round; c) Twelfth round

4 How many times did he fight his fierce welterweight rival from Cuba, Luis Rodriguez? a) Three times; b) Four times; c) Five times

5 Which British opponent did he stop in nine rounds at Wembley? a) Brian Curvis; b) Ralph Charles; c) Dave Charnley

6 In how many world title fights did he participate, including at welterweight, light-middle and middleweight? a) Sixteen; b) Twenty; c) Twenty-four

7 Where did he stop British middleweight Harry Scott in seven rounds? a) Liverpool; b) London; c) Las Vegas

8 From whom did he take the world middleweight title in 1966? a) Dick Tiger; b) Joey Giardello; c) Paul Pender

How many years did his career last?
a) 15; b) 17; c) 19

 How many fights did he have during his career?
a) 92; b) 102; c) 112

 How old was he when he had his final fight?
a) 37; b) 39; c) 41

 To whom did he lose two-one in a three-fight world middleweight title series? a) Rodrigo Valdez; b) Hugo Corro; c) Nino Benvenuti

 He dropped back down to welterweight to try to regain the world welterweight title from whom? a) Jose Napoles; b) Billy Backus; c) Curtis Cokes

 Where did he challenge Carlos Monzon for the world middleweight title? a) Mexico City; b) Buenos Aires; c) Monte Carlo

 Against which British boxer did he lose in the final fight of his career? a) John H. Stracey; b) Kevin Finnegan; c) Alan Minter

IN THIS CORNER
Marvin Hagler

Award yourself a points win if you get eight or more right. It's a draw if you get seven right. You win by a knockout if you get 12 or more right.

At which weight was he the national American amateur champion? a) Welterweight; b) Light-middleweight; c) Middleweight

What was the nickname that he adopted as an official part of his name? a) Magnificent Marvin; b) Marvelous Marvin; c) Macho Marvin

Who are the brothers who managed him throughout his career? a) Dundee brothers; b) Petronelli brothers; c) Duva brothers

Which former Olympic champion held him to a draw over 10 rounds in 1974? a) Emilio Correa; b) Ray Seales; c) Ronnie Harris

Which British opponent did he stop twice in two meetings in 1978? a) Bunny Sterling; b) Mark Rowe; c) Kevin Finnegan

What was the result of his first bid for the world title against Vito Antufermo? a) A draw; b) Lost on a disqualification; c) Lost on points

In which round did he stop Alan Minter when winning the world title at Wembley? a) Third round; b) Fifth round; c) Seventh round

Where did he successfully defend the title against Tony Sibson? a) Lewiston, Maine; b) Worcester, Massachusetts; c) Hartford, Connecticut

In which year did he make his professional debut?
a) 1969; b) 1971; c) 1973

 He became world champion after how many fights?
a) 34; b) 44; c) 54

 In which round did he stop Thomas Hearns in 1985?
a) Second; b) Third; c) Fourth

 How many successful defences of the middleweight title did he make? a) Twelve; b) Fourteen; c) Sixteen

 Who briefly floored Hagler before being stopped in the tenth round of a world title fight? a) Roberto Duran; b) Juan Roldan; c) Mustafa Hamsho

 In which round did he stop John Mugabi to retain the world middleweight title? a) Seventh round; b) Ninth round; c) Eleventh round

 Where was he outpointed in his showdown fight against Sugar Ray Leonard? a) Atlantic City; b) San Francisco; c) Las Vegas

SCORECARD

Points:

Result:

IN THIS CORNER

Len Harvey

Award yourself a points win if you get six or more right. It's a draw if you get five right. You win by a knockout if you get 10 or more right.

1 In which English county was he born and raised?
a) Kent; b) Derbyshire; c) Cornwall

2 How old was he when he made his professional debut?
a) Twelve; b) Thirteen; c) Fourteen

3 At what weight did he first challenge for a British championship? a) Lightweight; b) Welterweight; c) Middleweight

4 Who held him to a draw over 20 rounds in his first championship fight? a) Alf Mancini; b) Frank Moody; c) Harry Mason

5 How many fights did he have before winning his first British title? a) 69; b) 79; c) 89

6 After six successful defences, who took the British middleweight title from him? a) Jock McAvoy; b) Jack Hood; c) Jack Casey

7 Who did he outpoint to win the British Empire light-heavyweight title in 1934? a) Eddie Phillips; b) Glenn Moody; c) Larry Gains

8 In how many weight divisions did he challenge for the British championship? a) Three; b) Four; c) Five

In which year did he make his professional debut?
a) 1920; b) 1924; c) 1928

 For how many years did he box professionally?
a) 18; b) 22; c) 24

 How many professional fights did he have?
a) 113; b)123; c) 133

 Who outpointed him when he challenged for the world middleweight title? a) Solly Kreiger; b) Marcel Thil; c) Fred Apostoli

 Where did he challenge John Henry Lewis for the world light-heavyweight championship? a) London; b) New York; c) Paris

 Against whom did he have his final fight at White Hart Lane? a) Jack Petersen; b) Jack London; c) Freddie Mills

 In which round was he knocked out in his last contest?
a) Second round; b) Fourth round; c) Sixth round

SCORECARD

Points:

Result:

THE
BIG
FIGHT
QUIZ
No. 33

IN THIS CORNER

Tommy Hearns

Award yourself a points win if you get eight or more right. It's a draw if you get seven right. You win by a knockout if you get 12 or more right.

1 At which weight did he win the Golden Gloves championship? a) Light-welterweight; b) Welterweight; c) Light-middleweight

2 In which city has he been based throughout his professional career? a) Philadelphia; b) Cleveland; c) Detroit

3 What is his most popular ring nickname? a) Hammer Fist; b) Hit Man; c) Hurricane

4 Who has managed him throughout the peak years of his career? a) Emanuel Steward; b) Lou Duva; c) Jackie McCoy

5 In which round did he stop Pipino Cuevas to win the WBA welterweight championship? a) Second round; b) Fourth round; c) Sixth round

6 Where was his first title fight against Sugar Ray Leonard staged? a) Atlantic City; b) New York City; c) Las Vegas

7 Who did he outpoint to win the WBC light-middleweight championship? a) Fred Hutchings; b) Luigi Michillo; c) Wilfred Benitez

8 What colour shorts has he worn in all his major title fights? a) Black; b) Red; c) Gold

In which year did he make his professional debut?
a) 1975; b) 1977; c) 1979

 In which round was he knocked out by Marvin Hagler?
a) Second; b) Third; c) Fourth

 How many times was he taken the distance before his first world title fight?
a) Once; b) Twice; c) Three times

 Who did he knock out in one round to win the North American middleweight title? a) Doug DeWitt; b) James Shuler; c) Jeff McCracken

 In which year did he take the world light-heavyweight title from Dennis Andries? a) 1986; b) 1987; c) 1988

 He won a record fourth world championship by beating which middleweight champion? a) Juan Roldan; b) Frank Tate; c) John Mugabi

 Which promoter brought Hearns and Leonard together for a final showdown in 1989? a) Don King; b) Bob Arum; c) Donald Trump

---

SCORECARD

Points:

Result:

IN THIS CORNER

Larry Holmes

Award yourself a points win if you get eight or more right. It's a draw if you get seven right. You win by a knockout if you get 12 or more right.

In which American state was Larry Holmes born?
a) Ohio; b) Georgia; c) Colorado

What was his most popular ring nickname?
a) Larry The Lion; b) The Eastern Assassin; c) Man With A Mission

How many fights did he have before challenging for the world heavyweight championship? a) 27; b) 33; c) 37

Who did he outpoint to win the WBC version of the heavyweight title? a) John Tate; b) Leon Spinks; c) Ken Norton

Muhammad Ali retired at the end of which round against him in their championship contest? a) Eighth round; b) Tenth round; c) Twelfth round

How many successful title defences did he make (not including his unsanctioned defence against Marvis Frazier)? a) 15; b) 17; c) 19

What did he weigh when he first won the world heavyweight championship? a) 14 stone 9 pounds; b) 15 stone 9 pounds; c) 16 stone 9 pounds

Against which of these challengers did he get up off the canvas to win a title fight—a) Tex Cobb; b) Earnie Shavers; c) Lorenzo Zanon

In which year did he make his professional debut?
a) 1973; b) 1975; c) 1977

 How many contests did he have during his professional career?
a) 49; b) 51; c) 53

 How many times was he defeated? a) Twice; b) Three times; c) Four times

 In which round did he stop 'Great White Hope' Gerry Cooney? a) Ninth round; b) Eleventh round; c) Thirteenth round

 Where were both his contests with Michael Spinks staged?
a) Atlantic City; b) Los Angeles; c) Las Vegas

 What was the slogan on the back of his dressing gown for the Mike Tyson fight? a) Upset of the Century; b) Shock the World c) The Tyson Tamer

15 In which round was he knocked out by Tyson in their world title contest? a) Fourth round; b) Fifth round; c) Sixth round

SCORECARD

Points:

Result:

THE BIG FIGHT QUIZ No. 35

IN THIS CORNER

Lloyd Honeyghan

Award yourself a points win if you get eight or more right. It's a draw if you get seven right. You win by a knockout if you get 12 or more right.

1 Where was Lloyd Honeyghan born?
a) Jamaica; b) Elephant & Castle; c) Barbados

2 Who was his manager in the first phase of his professional career? a) Terry Lawless; b) Dennie Mancini; c) Al Phillips

3 Who was his manager when he became world welterweight champion? a) Mickey Duff; b) Mike Barrett; c) Bobby Neill

4 Who did he beat for the vacant British welterweight championship? a) Henry Rhiney; b) Kirkland Laing; c) Cliff Gilpin

5 Where did he beat Kevin Austin in his first overseas contest?
a) Chicago; b) Las Vegas; c) Atlantic City

6 Against which former stablemate did he win a fight in which three titles were at stake? a) Kirkland Laing; b) Sylvester Mittee; c) Maurice Hope

7 In which round did he stop Don Curry to win the world welterweight title? a) Sixth round; b) Eighth round; c) Tenth round

8 He gave up the WBA title rather than defend it against a challenger from which country? a) Cuba; b) Argentina; c) South Africa

In which year did he turn professional? a) 1978; b) 1980; c) 1982

 How many fights had he had when he earned a world title shot? a) 17; b) 27; c) 37

 Who ended his unbeaten record? a) Mark Breland; b) Jorge Vaca; c) Simon Brown

 In which round did he avenge his first defeat with a knockout victory at Wembley in 1988? a) Third round; b) Fifth round; c) Seventh round

 Who did he beat after landing a low blow in a controversial title defence in Atlantic City? a) Fujio Azaki; b) Sang-Ho Lee; c) Young-Kil Chung

 Who was appointed referee for his title fight showdown with Marlon Starling? a) Mills Lane; b) Richard Greene; c) Carlos Padilla

 In which round was he stopped by Starling in their welterweight title fight in 1989? a) Seventh round; b) Ninth round; c) Eleventh round

BIG FIGHT QUIZ No 34 ANSWERS

LARRY HOLMES: 1. Georgia; 2. The Eastern Assassin; 3. 27 fights; 4. Ken Norton; 5. Tenth round; 6. 19; 7. 14st 9lbs ; 8. Earnie Shavers; 9.1973; 10. 51; 11. Three times; 12. Thirteenth round; 13. Las Vegas; 14. Shock the World; 15. Fourth round.

SCORECARD

Points:

Result:

IN THIS CORNER
Maurice Hope

Award yourself a points win if you get seven or more right. It's a draw if you get six right. You win by a knockout if you get 11 or more right.

 Where was Maurice Hope born?
a) Guyana; b) Antigua; c) Leeward Isles

 What slogan did he always have on his dressing gown for major fights? a) Hope and Glory; b) Let's Go Mo; c) The Mowing Machine

 He won the British light-middleweight title after how many contests? a) Eleven; b) Seventeen; c) Twenty-one

 From whom did he take the championship with an eighth round victory? a) Larry Paul; b) Pat Thomas; c) Kevin White

 He won a Lonsdale Belt outright by beating which opponent? a) Bobby Arthur; b) Tony Poole; c) Albert Hillman

 In which round did Bunny Sterling stop him when he challenged for the British middleweight title? a) Eighth round; b) Tenth round; c) Twelfth round

 From whom did he take the European light-middleweight title? a) José Duran; b) Gilbert Cohen; c) Vito Antuofermo

 Where did he hold champion Eckhard Dagge to a draw in his first world title fight? a) Berlin; b) Dortmund; c) Munich

In which year did he make his professional debut?
a) 1971; b) 1973; c) 1975

 How many fights did he have as a professional?
a) 35; b) 45; c) 55

 In which round did he knock out Joel Bonnetaz in 1977?
a) Fourth; b) Fifth; c) Sixth

 Where did he challenge Rocky Mattioli for the world light-middleweight title? a) San Remo; b) Monte Carlo; c) Milan

 In which round did he stop Mattioli to win the championship?
a) Eighth round; b) Tenth round; c) Twelfth round

 Against which opponent did he make his first defence of the world title? a) Rocky Mattioli; b) Carlos Herrera; c) Mike Baker

 Who knocked him out in 12 rounds to take the world title off him in 1981? a) Roberto Duran; b) Wilfred Benitez; c) Ayub Kalule

BIG FIGHT QUIZ No 35 ANSWERS

LLOYD HONEYGHAN: 1. Jamaica; 2. Terry Lawless; 3. Mickey Duff; 4. Cliff Gilpen; 5. Chicago; 6. Sylvester Mittee; 7. Sixth round; 8. South Africa; 9. 1980; 10. 27 fights; 11. Jorge Vaca; 12. Third round; 13. Young-Kil Chung; 14. Mills Lane; 15. Ninth round.

SCORECARD

Points:

Result:

THE BIG FIGHT QUIZ No. 37

IN THIS CORNER

Ingemar Johansson

Award yourself a points win if you get seven or more right. It's a draw if you get six right. You win by a knockout if you get 11 or more right.

1 At which Olympics was he disqualified for allegedly not trying? a) London 1948; b) Helsinki 1952; b) Melbourne 1956

2 In which Swedish city was he born and raised? a) Stockholm; b) Malmo; c) Gothenburg

3 What name was given to his devastating right hand punch? a) The Goodnight Right; b) Ingo's Bingo; c) Mr Dynamite

4 Who was the first of his six British-based opponents? a) Peter Bates; b) Henry Cooper; c) Joe Bygraves

5 In which round did he stop Joe Erskine in defence of his European heavyweight title? a) Ninth round; b) Eleventh round; c) Thirteenth round

6 Which top contender did he knock out in one round to set up a world title fight? a) Eddie Machen; b) Cleveland Williams; c) Nino Valdes

7 Who was the referee for his first world title fight against Floyd Patterson? a) Arthur Donvan; b) Ruby Goldstein; c) Frank Sikora

8 How many times did he knock down Patterson in the third round of their first fight? a) Five times; b) Six times; c) Seven times

In which year did he make his professional debut?
a) 1950; b) 1952; c) 1954

 How many times was he beaten? a) Twice; b) Three times; c) Four times

 How many professional fights did he have?
a) 28; b) 38; c) 48

 In which round did Patterson knock him out to regain the world championship? a) Third round; b) Fifth round; c) Seventh round

 Where did he and Patterson meet for their final showdown? a) Miami Beach; b)Washington DC; c) San Francisco

 Who did he knock out in eight rounds to regain the European heavyweight title? a) Heinz Neuhaus; b) Dick Richardson; c) Francesco Cavicchi

 Who knocked him flat on his back in the final seconds of his last fight that he won on points? a) Wim Snoek; b) Hans Friedrich; c) Brian London

BIG FIGHT QUIZ No 36 ANSWERS

MAURICE HOPE: 1. Antigua; 2. Let's Go Mo; 3. Eleven contests; 4. Larry Paul; 5. Tony Poole; 6. Eighth round; 7. Vito Antuofermo; 8. Berlin; 9. 1973; 10. 35 fights; 11. Fifth round; 12. San Remo; 13. Eighth round; 14. Mike Baker; 15. Wilfred Benitez.

SCORECARD

Points:

Result:

THE BIG FIGHT QUIZ No. 38

IN THIS CORNER
Jack Johnson

Award yourself a points win if you get six or more right. It's a draw if you get five right. You win by a knockout if you get 10 or more right.

 1 In which American state was he born and raised?
a) Michigan; b) North Carolina; c) Texas

 2 What was his most popular ring nickname?
a) The Galveston Giant; b) The Black Tornado; c) The Ring Master

 3 What was his real first Christian name?
a) Archibald; b) Arthur; c) Albert

 4 How many years was he a professional before he got a crack at the world championship? a) Eight years; b) Ten years; c) Twelve years

 5 How many times did he fight his great rival Joe Jeanette before becoming world champion? a) Five times; b) Seven times; c) Nine times

 6 Where did he challenge Tommy Burns for the world heavyweight title? a) Sydney; b) Melbourne; c) Adelaide

 7 In which round did police stop his one-sided fight with Burns? a) Tenth round; b) Twelfth round; c) Fourteenth round

 8 Which middleweight champion knocked him down before being knocked out? a) Billy Papke; b) George Chip; c) Stanley Ketchel

84

In which year did he make his ring debut? a) 1897; b) 1907; c) 1917

 How many years did his professional career last? a) 21; b) 27; c) 31

 How many officially recorded contests did he have, not counting exhibition matches? a) 97; b) 107; c) 117

 Where did he retain his title with a 20 rounds points win against Frank Moran? a) Paris; b) Amsterdam; c) Madrid

 Which ex-champ came out of retirement to make an unsuccessful challenge against him? a) James J. Corbett; b) James J. Jeffries; c) John L. Sullivan

 Where did he lose his championship to Jess Willard? a) Quebec; b) Carson City; c) Havana

 In which round was he knocked out by Willard? a) Eighteenth round; b) Twenty-second round; c) Twenty-sixth round

IN THIS CORNER

Colin Jones

Award yourself a points win if you get seven or more right. It's a draw if you get six right. You win by a knockout if you get 11 or more right.

In which district of Wales was he born?
a) Aberavon; b) Gorseinon; c) Caerphilly

At which weight was he twice ABA champion?
a) Lightweight; b) Light-welterweight; c) Welterweight

How did he lose his 20-fight unbeaten record to Curtis Ramsey? a) He was disqualified; b) His eye was cut; c) He broke a bone in his hand

Who did he twice stop in the ninth round when behind on points in British title fights? a) Peter Neal; b) Billy Waith; c) Kirkland Laing

In which round did he beat Mark Harris for the vacant Commonwealth welterweight title? a) Fifth round; b) Seventh round; c) Ninth round

Which American did he knock out in one round in his first fight after winning the British title? a) Richard House; b) Milton Guest; c) Jerry Lewis

Where did he challenge Hans Henrik Palm for the European welterweight title? a) Cardiff; b) Copenhagen; c) Cologne

In which round did he stop Palm to become European champion? a) Second round; b) Seventh round; c) Eleventh round

In which year did he make his professional debut?
a) 1975; b) 1977; c) 1979

 Who was his manager?
a) Benny Jacobs; b) Eddie Thomas; c) Andy Smith

 Where was his first world title fight? a) Reno; b) New York; c) Seattle

 Who did he twice fight for the vacant WBC world welterweight title? a) Carlos Palomino; b) Milton McCrory; c) Sugar Ray Leonard

 Who did he stop in ten rounds before his third challenge for the world title? a) Allan Braswell; b) Pete Seward; c) Billy Parks

 Where did he challenge Don Curry for the WBA world welterweight championship? a) Birmingham; b) Cardiff; c) Manchester

 In which round was he stopped with a cut by Curry? a) Second round; b) Fourth round; c) Sixth round

THE BIG FIGHT QUIZ No. 40

IN THIS CORNER
Jake LaMotta

Award yourself a points win if you get six or more right. It's a draw if you get five right. You win by a knockout if you get 10 or more right.

 1 In which district of New York City was Jake LaMotta born and raised? a) Brooklyn; b) Richmond; c) The Bronx

 2 What was his real Christian name?
a) Giovanni; b) Giacobe; c) Giuseppe

 3 By what ring nickname was he popularly known?
a) The Bronx Bull; b) The Butcher of Brooklyn; c) The Richmond Wrecker

 4 What was the title of the film based on his life?
a) Rage In the Ring; b) An Age of Rage; c) Raging Bull

 5 Who portrayed LaMotta in the film? a) Robert DeNiro; b) Al Pacino; c) James Caan

 6 How many times did he and Sugar Ray Robinson meet as professionals? a) Four times; b) Five times; c) Six times

 7 How many years had he been a professional before he got a shot at the world title? a) Five years; b) Seven years; c) Nine years

 8 From which champion did he take the world middleweight title? a) Tony Zale; b) Marcel Cerdan; c) Rocky Graziano

In which year did he make his professional debut?
a) 1939; b) 1941; c) 1943

 How many fights did he have as a professional?
a) 96; b) 106; c) 116

 When did he make his final appearance before hanging up his gloves?
a) 1952; b) 1954; c) 1956

 Against which opponent did he make his first defence of the world title? a) Bobo Olson; b) Tony Zale; c) Tiberio Mitri

 Who did he knock out in the last minute of a world title fight when behind on points? a) Laurent Dauthuille; b) Robert Villemain; c) Bob Murphy

 In which round did Ray Robinson stop him in their final meeting for the world title? a) Eleventh round; b) Thirteenth round; c) Fifteenth round

 What new role did he take up with success after his retirement?
a) Nightclub entertainer; b) A tapdancer; c) A jazz singer

THE BIG FIGHT QUIZ No. 41

IN THIS CORNER

Sugar Ray Leonard

Award yourself a points win if you get eight or more right. It's a draw if you get seven right. You win by a knockout if you get 12 or more right.

 1 In which state in America was Ray Leonard born?
a) Maryland; b) South Carolina; c) Ohio

 2 At which weight was he an Olympic gold medallist?
a) Light-welterweight; b) Welterweight; c) Light-middle-weight

 3 In which Olympics did he win his gold medal?
a) Munich 1972; b) Montreal 1976; c) Moscow 1980

 4 Who ended his 27-fight unbeaten record as a professional?
a) Randy Shields; b) Roberto Duran; c) Larry Bonds

 5 Where did he challenge Wilfred Benitez for the world welterweight title? a) San Juan; b) Tucson; c) Las Vegas

 6 In which round did he stop Benitez to become the new world champion? a) Eleventh round; b) Thirteenth round; c) Fifteenth round

 7 Which British challenger did he knock out in four rounds?
a) Dave Green; b) John H. Stracey; c) Pat Thomas

 8 Where was his second fight with Roberto Duran staged?
a) Seattle; b) Houston; c) New Orleans

In which year did he make his professional debut?
a) 1973; b) 1977; c) 1980

 How many fights did he have before his first retirement?
a) 23; b) 33; c) 43

 In which round did he knock out Bruce Finch in 1982?
a) Third; b) Fourth; c) Fifth

 In which round did he stop Tommy Hearns in their welterweight title fight? a) Tenth round; b) Twelfth round; c) Fourteenth round

 What regular new role did he perform with success following his first retirement? a) TV commentator; b) Film actor; c) Male model

 How long had he been retired before he made a comeback to beat Marvin Hagler for the middleweight title? a) One year; b) Two years; c) Three years

How many rounds to win the WBC world light-heavyweight title in 1988? a) Virgil Hill; b) Leslie Stewart; c) Donny Lalonde

BIG FIGHT QUIZ No 40 ANSWERS

JAKE LAMOTTA: 1. The Bronx; 2. Giacobe; 3. The Bronx Bull; 4. Raging Bull; 5. Robert DeNiro; 6. Six times; 7. Nine years; 8. Marcel Cerdan; 9. 1941; 10. 106 fights; 11. 1954; 12. Tiberio Mitri; 13. Laurent Dauthuille; 14. Thirteenth round; 15. Nightclub entertainer.

SCORECARD

Points:

Result:

THE BIG FIGHT QUIZ No. 42

IN THIS CORNER
Ted 'Kid' Lewis

Award yourself a points win if you get six or more right. It's a draw if you get five right. You win by a knockout if you get 10 or more right.

1 Where was Ted 'Kid' Lewis born and raised?
a) East London; b) Manchester; c) Portsmouth

2 What was his real name?
a) Moishe Greenstock; b) Gershon Mendeloff; c) Jacob Finkelstein

3 How old was he when he made his professional debut?
a) Fourteen; b) Fifteen; c) Sixteen

4 At which weight did he win his first British championship?
a) Featherweight; b) Lightweight; c) Welterweight

5 How many major championships did he win during his extraordinary career? a) Seven b) Nine; c) Eleven

6 In which country did he fight five 20-round contests in 63 days? a) Canada; b) South Africa; c) Australia

7 How many times did he fight his great welterweight rival Jack Britton? a) Ten times; b) Fifteen times; c) Twenty times

8 Which ex-lightweight champion did he outpoint after becoming world welterweight champion? a) Willie Ritchie; b) Ad Wolgast; c) Joe Gans

How long did his ring career last? a) 15 years; b) 20 years; c) 25 years

 How many recorded fights did he have? a) 233; b) 253; c) 283

 Where did he fight Georges Carpentier? a) Paris; b) London; c) Brussels

 From whom did he take the British welterweight title on his return to England? a) Johnny Bee; b) Kid Doyle; c) Gus Platts

 In which round did he knock out Frankie Burns to win the Empire middleweight title? a) Ninth round; b) Eleventh round; c) Thirteenth round

 Against which future world champion was he disqualified in his final fight in the USA? a) Maxie Rosenbloom; b) Tommy Loughran; c) Lou Scozza

 Which old four-fight rival did he stop in three rounds in his final contest? a) Tommy Milligan; b) Augie Ratner; c) Johnny Basham

BIG FIGHT QUIZ No 41 ANSWERS

SUGAR RAY LEONARD: 1. South Carolina; 2. Light-welterweight; 3. Montreal 1976; 4. Roberto Duran; 5. Las Vegas; 6. Fifteenth; 7. Dave Green; 8. New Orleans; 9. 1977; 10. 33 fights; 11. Third; 12. Fourteenth; 13. TV commentator; 14. Three years; 15. Donny Lalonde.

SCORECARD

Points:

Result:

THE BIG FIGHT QUIZ No. 43

IN THIS CORNER

Sonny Liston

Award yourself a points win if you get seven or more right. It's a draw if you get six right. You win by a knockout if you get 11 or more right.

1 In which American state was Sonny Liston born? a) Illinois; b) Florida; c) Arkansas

2 What was his real Christian name? a) Charles; b) Leonard; c) Harold

3 By which ring nickname was he best known? a) Old Dynamite; b) Old Stone Face; c) Old Rockfist

4 Who was the only fighter to beat him before he won the world heavyweight title? a) Mike DeJohn; b) Willi Besmanoff; c) Marty Marshall

5 In which city did he have his first five professional fights? a) St Louis; b) Detroit; c) Washington DC

6 How many years after turning professional did he get his first shot at the world heavyweight title? a) Five years; b) Seven years; c) Nine years

7 In which round did he knock out Albert Westphal to set up a world title fight against Floyd Patterson? a) First round; b) Second round; c) Third round

8 Where was his first championship contest against Patterson staged? a) Miami Beach; b) Las Vegas; c) Chicago

94

In which year did he make his debut? a) 1953; b) 1955; c) 1957

 In which year did he have his final fight? a) 1966; b) 1968; c) 1970

 How many professional contests did he have? a) 34; b) 44; c) 54

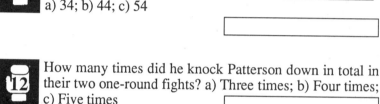

 How many times did he knock Patterson down in total in their two one-round fights? a) Three times; b) Four times; c) Five times

 Which ex-world champion refereed his second fight with Muhammad Ali? a) Rocky Marciano; b) Ezzard Charles; c) Jersey Joe Walcott

 In which country did he have four successive fights after his second defeat by Ali? a) Sweden; b) Mexico; c) Canada

Which title contender did he stop in 10 rounds in his final ring appearance? a) George Chuvalo; b) Thad Spencer; c) Chuck Wepner

SCORECARD

Points:

Result:

THE BIG FIGHT QUIZ No. 44

IN THIS CORNER

Joe Louis

Award yourself a points win if you get seven or more right.
It's a draw if you get six right. You win by a knockout if you
get 11 or more right.

 1 In which American state was Joe Louis born?
a) Alabama; b) Tennessee; c) Pennsylvania

 2 To what surname did he answer before becoming a professional boxer? a) Barrow; b) Lafayette; c) Brown

 3 At what weight was he national American amateur champion? a) Middleweight; b) Light-heavyweight; c) Heavyweight

 4 Which was the first former world champion that he beat before winning the title himself? a) Jack Sharkey; b) Max Baer; c) Primo Carnera

 5 Who was the only fighter to beat him on his way to winning the championship? a) King Levinsky; b) Max Schmeling; c) Paolino Uzcudun

 6 In which round did he knock out James J. Braddock to win the world heavyweight title? a) Fourth round; b) Sixth round; c) Eighth round

 7 Against which challenger did he make his first defence of the title? a) Tommy Farr; b) Nathan Mann; c) Harry Thomas

 8 Who was the referee for twelve of his championship defences? a) Ruby Goldstein; b) Frank Fullam; c) Arthur Donovan

In which year did he make his professional debut?
a) 1930; b) 1932; c) 1934

 In how many title fights did he participate?
a) 23; b) 25; c) 27

 In which year did he make his final ring appearance?
a) 1950; b) 1952; c) 1954

 Who was the first fighter to challenge him in two title fights?
a) Buddy Baer; b) Arturo Godoy; c) Abe Simon

In which round did he knock out Billy Conn in their return championship contest? a) Eighth round; b) Eleventh round; c) Thirteenth round

Which of his challengers boasted: 'I'll moider de bum!'?
a) Tami Mauriello; b) Tony Galento; c) Lou Nova

Who became only the second fighter to stop him in the final fight of his career? a) Jersey Joe Walcott; b) Ezzard Charles; c) Rocky Marciano

BIG FIGHT QUIZ No 43 ANSWERS

SONNY LISTON: 1. Arkansas; 2. Charles; 3. Old Stone Face; 4. Marty Marshall; 5. St Louis; 6. Nine years; 7. First round; 8. Chicago; 9. 1953; 10. 1970; 11. 54 fights; 12. Four times; 13. Jersey Joe Walcott; 14. Sweden; 15. Chuck Wepner.

SCORECARD

Points:

Result:

IN THIS CORNER
Benny Lynch

Award yourself a points win if you get six or more right. It's a draw if you get five right. You win by a knockout if you get 10 or more right.

1 In which Scottish district was he born and raised?
a) Paisley; b) Govan; c) Clydesdale

2 How old was he when he made his professional debut?
a) Sixteen; b) Seventeen; c) Eighteen

3 Who did he twice outpoint in fights for the Scottish flyweight title when he was 21? a) Jim Campbell; b) Jim Brady; c) Sandy McEwan

4 How many fights did he have in his busiest year?
a) 25 fights; b) 30 fights; c) 35 fights

5 Where did he challenge Jackie Brown for the world title in their second contest following a draw? a) Manchester; b) Glasgow; c) Newcastle

6 In which round did he force Brown to retire to win the British version of the world title? a) Second round; b) Fourth round; c) Sixth round

7 Who outpointed him over 12 rounds in a non-title fight in Belfast? a) Jim Brady; b) Jim Warnock; c) Jim Knowles

8 Who did he knock out in eight rounds to retain the British version of the world title? a) Evan Evans; b) Phil Milligan; c) Pat Palmer

98

In which year did he turn professional?
a) 1929; b) 1931; c) 1933

 How many fights did he have as a professional?
a) 102; b) 112; c) 122

 When did he make his final official ring appearance?
a) 1936; b) 1938; c) 1940

 In which round did he knock out Peter Kane in their first world title fight? a) Eleventh round; b) Thirteenth round; c) Fifteenth round

 Who did he outpoint to become the undisputed champion of the world? a) Small Montana; b) Young Perez; c) Newsboy Brown

 How many pounds was he overweight for his fight against Jackie Jurich when he was forced to forfeit his title? a) Four; b) Six; c) Eight

 Who stopped him in five rounds in the final fight of his career? a) Maurice Filhol; b) Fortunato Ortega; c) Aurel Toma

BIG FIGHT QUIZ No 44 ANSWERS

JOE LOUIS: 1. Alabama; 2. Barrow; 3. Middleweight; 4. Primo Carnera; 5. Max Schmeling; 6. Eighth round; 7. Tommy Farr; 8. Arthur Donovan; 9. 1934; 10. 27 title fights; 11. 1950; 12. Arturo Godoy; 13. Eighth round; 14. Tony Galento; 15. Rocky Marciano.

SCORECARD

Points:

Result:

THE BIG FIGHT QUIZ No. 46

IN THIS CORNER

Walter McGowan

Award yourself a points win if you get seven or more right. It's a draw if you get six right. You win by a knockout if you get 11 or more right.

In which district in Scotland was Walter McGowan born ?
a) Burnbank; b) Auchterader; c) Hamilton

At which weight did he win an ABA championship?
a) Light-flyweight; b) Flyweight; c) Bantamweight

What relation was his manager Joe Gans to him?
a) Father; b) Uncle; c) Brother-in-law

How many professional fights did he have before challenging for the British flyweight championship? a) Nine fights; c) Twelve fights; c) Twenty

From whom did he take the British and Commonwealth flyweight titles? a) John Caldwell; b) Frankie Jones; c) Jackie Brown

Where was he outpointed in his first challenge for the European flyweight championship? a) Paris; b) Rome; c) Berlin

Who held him to a draw when he made a bid for the European bantamweight title? a) Tommaso Galli; b) Franco Zurlo; c) Salvatore Fabrizio

From whom did he take the world flyweight title at Wembley?
a) Hiroyuki Ebihara; b) Pone Kingpetch; c) Salvatore Burruni

In which year did he make his professional debut?
a) 1957; b) 1959; c) 1961

 How many professional fights did he have?
a) 30; b) 40; c) 50

 In which year did he have his final contest?
a) 1969; b) 1971; c) 1973

 From whom did he take the British and Commonwealth bantamweight titles? a) Johnny Clark; b) Alan Rudkin; c) Dave Needham

 Where did he lose his world flyweight title to Chartchai Chionoi? a) Bangkok; b) Pnompenh; c) Manila

 In which round did Chionoi stop him with a cut eye in their return world title fight at Wembley? a) Seventh round; b) Ninth round; c) Twelfth round

Where did he lose his British and Commonwealth bantamweight titles to Alan Rudkin? a) Liverpool; b) Glasgow; c) Manchester

BIG FIGHT QUIZ No 45 ANSWERS

SCORECARD

Points:

Result:

IN THIS CORNER

Barry McGuigan

Award yourself a points win if you get eight or more right. It's a draw if you get seven right. You win by a knockout if you get 12 or more right.

 How old was Barry McGuigan when he won a Commonwealth Games gold medal? a) Seventeen; b) Eighteen; c) Nineteen

 At which weight was he Commonwealth Games champion? a) Flyweight; b) Bantamweight; c) Featherweight

 Who was his manager in the first phase of his professional career? a) Frank Warren; b) Mike Barrett; c) Barney Eastwood

 What is his most popular ring nickname? a) The Clones Cyclone; b) King Barry; c) Perpetual Motion

 Who was the only fighter to beat him before he became world champion? a) Juan LaPorte; b) Charm Chiteule; c) Peter Eubanks

 In which round did he stop Vernon Penprase to win the vacant British featherweight title? a) Second round; b) Fourth round; c) Sixth round

 Who did he beat for the vacant European featherweight title? a) Jose Caba; b) Ruben Herasme; c) Valerio Nati

 At which London football ground did he challenge for the world featherweight title? a) Loftus Road; b) White Hart Lane; c) Highbury Stadium

How many fights did he have before becoming world champion?
a) 27; b) 30; c) 33

 In which year did he turn professional?
a) 1979; b) 1980; c) 1981

 In which round did he floor Eusebio Pedroza?
a) Seventh; b) Eighth; c) Ninth

 Who did he stop in eight rounds in his first defence of the world title? a) Ki-Yung Chung; b) Bernard Taylor; c) Rocky Lockridge

 Where did he stop Danilo Cabrera in a second world title defence? a) Belfast; b) Wembley; c) Dublin

 Who beat him on points to capture the world featherweight title? a) Antonio Rivera; b) Lupe Pintor; c) Steve Cruz

 Who did he beat in his first comeback contest after losing the world title? a) Nicky Perez; b) Harold Knight; c) Marcos Villasana

SCORECARD

Points:

Result:

THE BIG FIGHT QUIZ No. 48

IN THIS CORNER

Charlie Magri

Award yourself a points win if you get seven or more right. It's a draw if you get six right. You win by a knockout if you get 11 or more right.

In which country was Charlie Magri born?
a) Algeria; b) Tunisia; c) Turkey

How many successive ABA championships did he win before turning professional? a) Two; b) Three; c) Four

Who managed him throughout his professional career?
a) George Francis; b) Andy Smith; c) Terry Lawless

Where in London was he based when he started his boxing career? a) Stepney; b) Bermondsey; c) Peckham

He won the British flyweight championship after how many fights? a) Three; b) Five; c) Seven

Who did he beat for the vacant British championship?
a) Tony Barlow; b) Tony Davies; c) Dave Smith

From whom did he take the European flyweight title in his twelfth professional fight? a) Fritz Chervet; b) Franco Udella; c) Rene Libeer

Who was the first opponent to beat him after a run of 23 unbeaten fights? a) Juan Diaz; b) Alfonso Lopez; c) Manuel Carrasco

In which year did he make his professional debut?
a) 1975; b) 1977; c) 1979

 In which year did he have his final fight?
a) 1984; b) 1985; c) 1986

 How many professional contests did he have?
a) 35; b) 45; c) 55

 What nationality was Eleoncio Mercedes, from whom he took the world flyweight title? a) Argentinian; b) Chilean; c) Dominican

 In which round was he stopped by Frank Cedeno when he lost his world title in his first defence? a) Fourth round; b) Sixth round; c) Eighth round

 Against whom did he make a second bid to win a world championship? a) Gabriel Bernal; b) Sot Chitalada; c) Koji Kobayashi

Duke McKenzie stopped him in how many rounds in the final fight of his career? a) Fifth round; b) Seventh round; c) Ninth round

IN THIS CORNER

Rocky Marciano

Award yourself a points win if you get eight or more right. It's a draw if you get seven right. You win by a knockout if you get 12 or more right.

1 What was Rocky Marciano's hometown, which formed part of his ring nickname? a) Brooklyn; b) Brockton; c) Brownsville

2 Who was his manager throughout his career? a) Cus D'Amato; b) Felix Bocchicchio; c) Al Weill

3 In which year did he make his professional debut? a) 1947; b) 1949; c) 1951

4 How many times was he taken the distance in championship and non-championship contests? a) Twice; b) Four times; c) Six times

5 In which round did he stop Joe Louis in their non-title fight in 1951? a) Sixth round; b) Eighth round; c) Tenth round

6 Who was his final opponent before he challenged for the world championship? a) Lee Savold; b) Rex Layne; c) Harry Matthews

7 In which round did he knock out Jersey Joe Walcott to win the world title? a) Ninth round; b) Eleventh; c) Thirteenth round

8 Against which opponent did Rocky suffer a badly gashed nose in a title fight? a) Ezzard Charles; b) Don Cockell; c) Jersey Joe Walcott

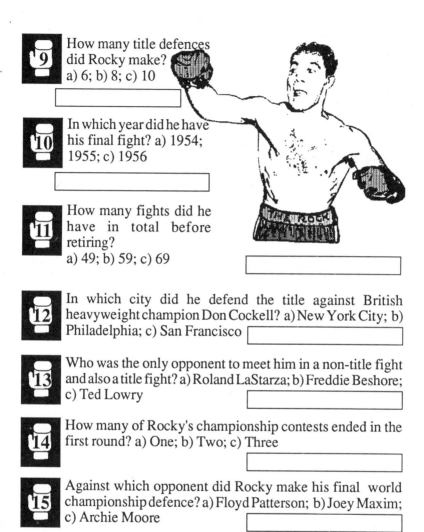

9 How many title defences did Rocky make? a) 6; b) 8; c) 10

10 In which year did he have his final fight? a) 1954; 1955; c) 1956

11 How many fights did he have in total before retiring? a) 49; b) 59; c) 69

12 In which city did he defend the title against British heavyweight champion Don Cockell? a) New York City; b) Philadelphia; c) San Francisco

13 Who was the only opponent to meet him in a non-title fight and also a title fight? a) Roland LaStarza; b) Freddie Beshore; c) Ted Lowry

14 How many of Rocky's championship contests ended in the first round? a) One; b) Two; c) Three

15 Against which opponent did Rocky make his final world championship defence? a) Floyd Patterson; b) Joey Maxim; c) Archie Moore

SCORECARD

Points:

Result:

THE BIG FIGHT QUIZ No. 50

IN THIS CORNER
Terry Marsh

Award yourself a points win if you get six or more right. It's a draw if you get five right. You win by a knockout if you get 10 or more right.

1 In which district of London was he born and raised?
a) Stepney; b) Rotherhithe; c) Blackfriars

2 At which weight did he win two ABA championships?
a) Lightweight; b) Light-welterweight; c) Welterweight

3 In which branch of the armed forces was he serving during his peak years as an amateur? a) Royal Air Force; b) Army; c) Royal Marines

4 What job was he holding down for most of his professional career? a) Traffic warden; b) Ambulanceman; c) Fireman

5 Who was his manager when he became champion of the world? a) Frank Warren; b) Brendan Ingle; c) Harry Holland

6 Who did he outpoint for the British light-welterweight championship at Shoreditch? a) Colin Power; b) Clinton McKenzie; c) Joey Singleton

7 Where did he win the vacant European light-welterweight championship? a) Milan; b) Barcelona; c) Monte Carlo

8 In which round did he knock out Alessandro Scapecchi to win the European title? a) Sixth round; b) Eighth round; c) Tenth round

108

In which year did he turn professional?
a) 1979; b) 1980 c) 1981

 Which version of the world championship did he win?
a) WBC; b) WBA; c) IBF

 Where did he challenge for the title? a) Luton; b) Watford; c) Basildon

 From whom did he take the world light-welterweight championship? a) Joe Louis Manley; b) Johnny Bumphus; c) Gary Hinton

 In which round did he win his first world championship contest? a) Tenth round; b) Twelfth round; c) Fourteenth round

 Who did he stop in six rounds in his first defence of the world championship? a) Meldrick Taylor; b) James McGirt; c) Akio Kameda

 What was the well publicised reason for his premature retirement from boxing? a) Damaged eye; b) Brittle bones; c) Epilepsy

BIG FIGHT QUIZ No 49 ANSWERS

ROCKY MARCIANO: 1. Brockton; 2. Al Weill; 3. 1947; 4. Six times; 5. Eighth round; 6. Harry Matthews; 7. Thirteenth round; 8. Ezzard Charles; 9. Six defences; 10. 1955; 11. 49; 12. San Francisco; 13. Roland LaStarza; 14. One; 15. Archie Moore.

SCORECARD

Points:

Result:

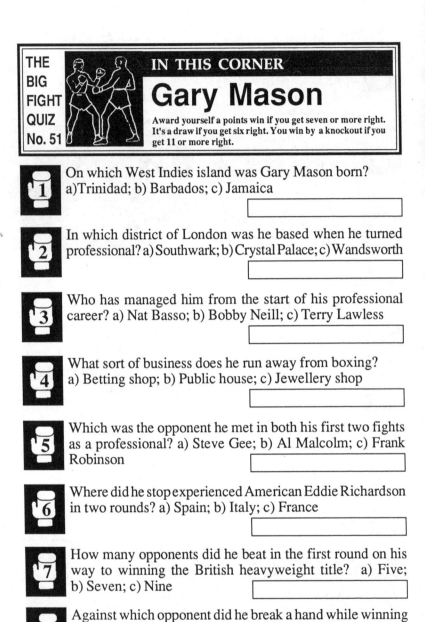

IN THIS CORNER

Gary Mason

Award yourself a points win if you get seven or more right. It's a draw if you get six right. You win by a knockout if you get 11 or more right.

1 On which West Indies island was Gary Mason born? a)Trinidad; b) Barbados; c) Jamaica

2 In which district of London was he based when he turned professional? a) Southwark; b) Crystal Palace; c) Wandsworth

3 Who has managed him from the start of his professional career? a) Nat Basso; b) Bobby Neill; c) Terry Lawless

4 What sort of business does he run away from boxing? a) Betting shop; b) Public house; c) Jewellery shop

5 Which was the opponent he met in both his first two fights as a professional? a) Steve Gee; b) Al Malcolm; c) Frank Robinson

6 Where did he stop experienced American Eddie Richardson in two rounds? a) Spain; b) Italy; c) France

7 How many opponents did he beat in the first round on his way to winning the British heavyweight title? a) Five; b) Seven; c) Nine

8 Against which opponent did he break a hand while winning in seven rounds? a) David Jaco; b) Manuel Almeida; c) Richard Scott

110

In which year did he make his professional debut?
a) 1983; b) 1984; c) 1985

 He won the British title after how many fights?
a) 19; b) 29; c) 39

 In which round did he stop James Tillis? a) Third;
b) Fifth; c) Seventh

 Who was the only opponent to go the distance with him before his title victory? a) Oscar Holman; b) Louis Perguad; c) Maurice Gomis

 Who did he meet for the vacant British heavyweight championship? a) Funso Banjo; b) Trevor Currie; c) Derrick Williams

 In which round did he win by a knockout to capture the British title? a) Fourth round; b) Sixth round; c) Eighth round

 Who did he beat in his first fight after becoming British champion? a) Harry Terrell; b) Terry Armstrong; c) Alfonzo Ratliff

BIG FIGHT QUIZ No 50 ANSWERS

TERRY MARSH: 1. Stepney; 2. Welterweight; 3. Royal Marines; 4. Fireman; 5. Frank Warren; 6. Clinton McKenzie; 7. Monte Carlo; 8. Sixth round; 9. 1981; 10. IBF; 11. Basildon; 12. Joe Louis Manley; 13. Tenth round; 14. Akio Kameda; 15. Epilepsy.

SCORECARD

Points:

Result:

THE BIG FIGHT QUIZ No. 52

IN THIS CORNER
Freddie Mills

Award yourself a points win if you get six or more right. It's a draw if you get five right. You win by a knockout if you get 10 or more right.

1 In which English county was he born and raised?
a) Somerset; b) Dorset; c) Hampshire

2 What job did he have during the early years of his boxing career? a) Postman; b) Farm worker; c) Milkman

3 Who was his manager throughout the peak years of his professional career? a) Ted Broadribb; b) Jim Wicks; c) Jack Burns

4 In which town did he have 42 of his first 50 fights?
a) Southampton; b) Bournemouth; c) Torquay

5 How many years had he been a professional before he fought Len Harvey for the British light-heavyweight title? a) Five; b) Seven; c) Nine

6 Who did he stop in one round to set up his title challenge against Harvey? a) Jock McAvoy; b) Eddie Phillips; c) Jack Petersen

7 In which branch of the armed forces was he serving when first reaching title class? a) Royal Air Force; b) Army; c) Royal Navy

8 Who outpointed him in a contest for the vacant British heavyweight championship? a) Ben Foord; b) George Cook; c) Jack London

112

In which year did he make his professional debut?
a) 1932; b) 1934; c) 1936

 How many professional fights did he have?
a) 87; b) 97; c) 107

 In which year did he have his final fight?
a) 1950; b) 1952; c) 1956

 In which round was he stopped in his first bid for the world light-heavyweight championship? a) Eighth round; b) Tenth round; c) Twelfth round

 Who did he outpoint to win the world title in a return contest? a) Billy Conn; b) Melio Bettina; c) Gus Lesnevich

 Which British heavyweight champion stopped him twice, once with the title at stake? a) Jack Gardner; b) Johnny Williams; c) Bruce Woodcock

 Who stopped him in the tenth round of his final fight to take his world title? a) Joey Maxim; b) Harold Johnson; c) Archie Moore

BIG FIGHT QUIZ No 51 ANSWERS

GARY MASON: 1. Jamaica; 2. Wandsworth; 3. Terry Lawless; 4. Jewellery shop; 5. Al Malcolm; 6. Spain; 7. Nine; 8. Manuel Almeida; 9. 1984; 10. 29 fights; 11. Fifth round; 12. Oscar Holman; 13. Trevor Currie; 14. Fourth round; 15. Terry Armstrong.

SCORECARD

Points:

Result:

THE BIG FIGHT QUIZ No. 53

IN THIS CORNER

ALAN MINTER

Award yourself a points win if you get seven or more right. It's a draw if you get six right. You win by a knockout if you get 11 or more right.

In which Olympics did Alan Minter win a bronze medal?
a) Mexico 1968; b) Munich 1972; c) Montreal 1976

In which English county was he born and raised?
a) Surrey; b) Sussex; c) Norfolk

What relation was his manager Doug Bidwell to him?
a) Brother-in-law; b) Father-in-law; c) Uncle

Who did he outpoint three times in fights for the British middleweight title? a) Kevin Finnegan; b) Bunny Sterling; c) Mark Rowe

In which round did he stop Billy Knight in his first defence of the British title? a) Second round; b) Fourth round; c) Sixth round

Which former Olympic champion did he stop in five rounds?
a) Ronnie Harris; b) Dieter Kottysch; c) Ray Seales

Where did he beat Germano Valsecchi for the European middleweight title? a) Milan; b) Rome; c) San Remo

In which round was he stopped by Gratien Tonna when he lost the European middleweight title? a) Fourth round; b) Sixth round; c) Eighth round

114

In which year did he make his professional debut?
a) 1968; b) 1972; c) 1976

 In which year did he have his final fight?
a) 1981; b) 1982; c) 1983

 How many professional contests did he have?
a) 39; b) 49; c) 59

 Where did he outpoint Vito Antuofermo for the world middleweight title? a) Jersey City; b) Las Vegas; c) Boston

 In which round did he stop Antuofermo in their return world title fight? a) Eighth round; b) Tenth round; c) Twelfth round

 Who was the referee for the fight in which he lost his world title to Marvin Hagler? a) Octavio Meyran; b) Ernesto Magana; c) Carlos Berrocal

 Who stopped him in three rounds in the final fight of his career? a) Mustafa Hamsho; b) Tony Sibson; c) Hugo Corro

SCORECARD

Points:

Result:

THE BIG FIGHT QUIZ No. 54

IN THIS CORNER
Rinty Monaghan

Award yourself a points win if you get six or more right. It's a draw if you get five right. You win by a knockout if you get 10 or more right.

1. What was Rinty Monaghan's hometown in Ireland?
a) Belfast; b) Newry; c) Armagh

2. How old was he when he made his professional debut?
a) Fourteen; b) Fifteen; c) Sixteen

3. What was his most popular ring nickname?
a) The Irish Imp; b) The Tiny Terror; c) The Singing Irishman

4. Who outpointed him in a rubber match at Liverpool after they had won one fight each? a) Cyclone Kelly; b) Joe Curran; c)Tommy Burney

5. How long had he been a professional before he made his debut in London? a) Eight years; b) Ten years; c) Twelve years

6. Who did he stop in one round in his first ring appearance in London? a) Terry Allen; b) Tommy Stewart; c) Sammy Reynolds

7. How did he lose his first fight against Dado Marino?
a) On a cut eye; b) On a disqualification; c) On a disputed points decision

8. Marino, beaten by Rinty for the NBA version of the world flyweight title, was from which country? a) Philippines; b) Hawaii; c) Tunisia

116

In which year did he make his professional debut?
a) 1935; b) 1937; c) 1939

 How many professional fights did he have?
a) 54; b) 64; c) 74

 In which year did he have his final fight? a) 1947; 1949; c) 1951

 In which round did he stop Jackie Paterson to become the undisputed champion of the world? a) Fifth round; b) Seventh round; c) Ninth round

 Who did he stop in seven rounds in his first fight after becoming undisputed champion? a) Charlie Squire; b) Otello Belardinelli; c) Ike Weir

 Where did he make a successful challenge for the European flyweight title against Maurice Sandeyron? a) Cherbourg; b) Manchester; c) Belfast

 How did the final contest of his career—a triple title fight against Terry Allen—end? a) In a points defeat; b) In a draw; c) In a points victory

SCORECARD

Points:

Result:

THE BIG FIGHT QUIZ No. 55

IN THIS CORNER
Carlos Monzon

Award yourself a points win if you get seven or more right. It's a draw if you get six right. You win by a knockout if you get 11 or more right.

 1 In which South American country was he born and raised? a) Colombia; b) Panama; c) Argentina

 2 At which weight did he make his professional debut? a) Welterweight; b) Light-middleweight; c) Middleweight

 3 After three defeats early in his career, how long did he go without being beaten? a) Nine years; b) Eleven years; c) Thirteen years

 4 How many fights did he have before challenging for the world middleweight championship? a) 61 fights; b) 71 fights; c) 81 fights

 5 Where did he make a successful challenge for the world title against Nino Benvenuti? a) Rome; b) New York; c) Paris

 6 In which round did he beat Benvenuti in their return title fight? a) Third round; b) Fifth round; c) Seventh round

 7 Which American did he stop in 14 rounds in his first defence of the title in his home town? a) Denny Moyer; b) Bennie Briscoe; c) Emile Griffith

 8 Who was the Frenchman who twice challenged him for the title in Paris? a) Gratian Tonna; b) Jean-Claude Bouttier; c) André Drille

In which year did he turn professional?
a) 1961; b) 1963 c) 1965

 How many professional fights did he have?
a) 101; b) 111; c) 121

 How many successful defences of the world title did he make during his long reign as champion?
a)12; b) 14; c) 16

 Which former world welterweight champion did he stop in seven rounds in Paris? a) Jose Napoles; b) Billy Backus; c) Carlos Palomino

 In which round did he stop Tony Licata when defending his title in New York? a) Eighth round; b) Tenth round; c) Twelfth round

 Where did he make the final two title defences of his career?
a) Monte Carlo; b) San Remo; c) Copenhagen

 Against which opponent did he twice successfully defend his title before retiring? a) Tom Bogs; b) Tony Mundine; c) Rodrigo Valdez

SCORECARD

Points:

Result:

THE BIG FIGHT QUIZ No. 56

IN THIS CORNER
Archie Moore

Award yourself a points win if you get seven or more right. It's a draw if you get six right. You win by a knockout if you get 11 or more right.

1 In which American state was he born?
a) Tennessee; b) Nevada; c) Mississippi

2 What was his name before he became a professional boxer?
a) Archibald Wilson; b) Archibald Wright; c) Archibald Williams

3 What was his first popular ring nickname?
a) The Mongoose; b) The Terminator; c) The Black Bull

4 What was his second popular ring nickname?
a) Ancient Archie; b) Old Man River; c) Ageless Archie

5 How many years was he a professional before he got his first shot at a world title? a) Thirteen years; b) Fifteen years; c) Seventeen years

6 In which country did he have seven of his eight fights in 1940? a) Mexico; b) South Africa; c) Australia

7 From whom did he take the world light-heavyweight championship? a) Harold Johnson; b) Gus Lesnevich; c) Joey Maxim

8 Against whom did he defend the title in his only ring appearance in London? a) Randolph Turpin; b) Yolande Pompey; c) Alex Buxton

120

In which year did he make his professional debut? a) 1932; b) 1934; c) 1936

 How many fights is he reputed to have had? a) 214; b) 224; c) 234

 How many fights did he win inside the distance? a) 125; b) 135; c) 145

 In which round did he beat Carl (Bobo) Olson in defence of his world light-heavyweight title? a) Third round; b) Fifth round; c) Seventh round

 Where did he challenge Rocky Marciano for the world heavyweight title? a) Philadelphia; b) Chicago; c) New York City

 In which round did Floyd Patterson knock him out to win the vacant world championship? a) Fifth round; b) Seventh round; c) Ninth round

 How old did the record books show him to be when he was beaten by Cassius Clay? a) 40; b) 44; c) 48

BIG FIGHT QUIZ No 55 ANSWERS

CARLOS MONZON: 1. Argentina; 2. Light-middleweight; 3. Thirteen years; 4. 81 fights; 5. Rome; 6. Third round; 7. Emile Griffith; 8. Jean-Claude Bouttier; 9. 1963; 10. 101 fights; 11. Fourteen defences; 12. Jose Napoles; 13. Tenth round; 14. Monte Carlo; 15. Rodrigo Valdez.

SCORECARD

Points:

Result:

121

IN THIS CORNER

Jose Napoles

Award yourself a points win if you get six or more right. It's a draw if you get five right. You win by a knockout if you get 10 or more right.

 Where was Jose Napoles born and raised?
a) Bolivia; b) Cuba; c) Venezuela

 At what weight did he make his professional debut?
a) Lightweight; b) Light-welterweight; c) Welterweight

 He had a Spanish nickname that meant as smooth as what?
a) Silk; b) Butter; c) Satin

From whom did he take the world welterweight championship? a) Curtis Cokes; b) Emile Griffith; c) Charlie Shipes

From whom did he regain the title after losing it on a cut eye defeat? a) Hedgemon Lewis; b) Ernie Lopez; c) Billy Backus

 In which round did he knock out British champion Ralph Charles at Wembley? a) Seventh round; b) Ninth round; c) Eleventh round

 Where did he successfully defend his world title against Commonwealth champion Clyde Gray? a) Melbourne; b) Toronto; c) Kingston

 Who did he stop in two rounds in a world title defence in Monterrey? a) Esteban Osuna; b) Roger Menetrey; c) Adolph Pruitt

In which year did he make his debut? a) 1954; b) 1956; c) 1958

 How many professional fights did he have? a) 74; b) 84; c) 94

 In which year did he have his final fight? a) 1975; b) 1977; c) 1979

 How many times did he emerge the winner in world title fights? a) Twelve times; b) Fourteen times; c) Sixteen times

 How old was he when he agreed to defend his title against British challenger John H. Stracey? a) Thirty-three; b) Thirty-five; c) Thirty-seven

 Where did he defend the championship against Stracey? a) Acapulco; b) Tijuana; c) Mexico City

 In which round was he stopped by Stracey in the final fight of his career? a) Sixth round; b) Eighth round; c) Tenth round

BIG FIGHT QUIZ No 51 ANSWERS

ARCHIE MOORE: 1. Mississippi; 2. Archibald Wright; 3. The Mongoose; 4. Ageless Archie; 5. Seventeen years; 6. Australia; 7. Joey Maxim; 8. Yolande Pompey; 9. 1936; 10. 234 fights; 11. 145 fights; 12. Third round; 13. New York City; 14. Fifth round; 15. 48 years old.

SCORECARD

Points:

Result:

THE BIG FIGHT QUIZ No. 58

IN THIS CORNER
Ken Norton

Award yourself a points win if you get seven or more right. It's a draw if you get six right. You win by a knockout if you get 11 or more right.

1 In which American state was Ken Norton born?
a) Missouri; b) Illinois; c) Ohio

2 Which out-of-the-ring career did he follow while boxing as a professional? a) Film acting; b) Sports commentator; c) Male model

3 In which American state did he have all but one of his first 32 fights? a) Florida; b) California; c) Texas

4 Where did he challenge George Foreman for the world heavyweight championship? a) Caracas; b) Panama City; c) Rio de Janeiro

5 In which round did Foreman stop him to retain the championship? a) Second round; b) Fourth round; c) Sixth round

6 Who did he outpoint in the fight before being proclaimed world heavyweight champion? a) Jerry Quarry; b) Larry Middleton; c) Jimmy Young

7 Where was he outpointed by Larry Holmes in a fight for the WBC version of the heavyweight title? a) New York; b) Chicago; c) Las Vegas

8 How many times did he meet Muhammad Ali?
a) Twice; b) Three times; c) Four times

In which year did he make his professional debut?
a) 1963; b) 1965; c) 1967

 In which year did he have his final fight?
a) 1981; b) 1982; c) 1983

 How many professional contests did he have?
a) 40; b) 50; c) 60

 In which round was he knocked out by Earnie Shavers?
a) First round; b) Second round; c) Third round

 Who held him to a draw over 10 rounds in Bloomington?
a) Mike Weaver; b) Scott LeDoux; c) Lorenzo Zanon

 How many of his fights did he win inside the distance?
a) Thirty-three; b) Thirty-six; c) Thirty-nine

 Who stopped him in one round to force his decision to retire from boxing? a) Trevor Berbick; b) Renaldo Snipes; c) Gerry Cooney

SCORECARD

Points:

Result:

THE BIG FIGHT QUIZ No. 59

IN THIS CORNER

Floyd Patterson

Award yourself a points win if you get seven or more right. It's a draw if you get six right. You win by a knockout if you get 11 or more right.

1 In which American state was Floyd Patterson born?
a) North Carolina; b) New York; c) Oregon

2 At which weight did he win an Olympic gold medal?
a) Middleweight; b) Light-heavyweight; c) Heavyweight

3 How old was he when he made his professional debut?
a) Seventeen; b) Eighteen; c) Nineteen

4 Who was his manager in the peak years of his professional career? a) Al Weill; b) Yancy Durham; c) Cus D'Amato

5 Who was the former world light-heavyweight champion who was the first man to beat him? a) Gus Lesnevich; b) Joey Maxim; c) Harold Johnson

6 Who did he outpoint over 12 rounds to clinch a shot at the vacant world title? a) Jimmy Slade; b) George Chuvalo; c) Tommy Jackson

7 Where did he beat Archie Moore to become the youngest world champion? a) New York City; b) Chicago; c) Los Angeles

8 In which round did he stop Tommy Jackson in his first defence of the championship? a) Sixth round; b) Eighth round; c) Twelfth round

In which year did he make his professional debut?
a) 1948; b) 1950; c) 1952

 How many professional fights did he have?
a) 64; b) 74; c) 84

 In which year did he have his final fight? a) 1970;
1972; c) 1974

 Which Olympic champion made his professional debut against him in a world title fight? a) Pete Rademacher; b) Ed Sanders; c) Norvel Lee

 In which round did he knock out Ingemar Johansson in their third and final meeting? a) Fourth round; b) Sixth round; c) Eighth round

 Where was he outpointed by Jimmy Ellis in a fight for the WBA heavyweight championship? a) Copenhagen; b) Helsinki; c) Stockholm

 Who stopped him in seven rounds in the final fight of his career? a) Jerry Quarry; b) Muhammad Ali; c) Oscar Bonavena

SCORECARD

Points:

Result:

THE BIG FIGHT QUIZ No. 60

IN THIS CORNER
Jack Petersen

Award yourself a points win if you get six or more right. It's a draw if you get five right. You win by a knockout if you get 10 or more right.

1 Where in Wales was Jack Petersen born and raised?
a) Cardiff; b) Swansea; c) Newport

2 At which weight was he an ABA champion?
a) Middleweight; b) Light-heavyweight; c) Heavyweight

3 How long had he been a professional before he won his first British title? a) Six months; b) Eight months; c) Ten months

4 Who did he outpoint to win the British light-heavyweight championship? a) Frank Moody; b) Gipsy Daniels; c) Harry Crossley

5 How many weeks later did he win the British heavyweight championship? a) Seven weeks; b) Nine weeks; c) Eleven weeks

6 In which round did he knock out Reggie Meen to become British heavyweight champion? a) Second round; b) Fourth round; c) Fifth round

7 Who did he knock out in 12 rounds in his first defence of the British heavyweight title? a) Phil Scott; b) Charlie Smith; c) Jack Pettifer

8 Who was disqualified against him in the second round when he won a Lonsdale Belt outright? a) Jack Doyle; b) George Cook; c) Ben Foord

128

In which year did he turn professional?
a) 1929; b) 1931; c) 1933

How many professional fights did he have?
a) 38; b) 48; c) 58

In which year did he have the final fight of his career before serving boxing in an administrative capacity?
a) 1935; b) 1937; c) 1939

In which round did he force Larry Gains to retire in a British Empire championship contest? a)Eleventh; b)Thirteenth; c) Fifteenth

Who did he beat twice and lose to once in British title fights?
a) Len Harvey; b) Jock McAvoy; c) Eddie Phillips

Where did he lose the British and Empire championships to Ben Foord? a) Nottingham; b) Liverpool; c) Leicester

He retired from the ring after losing his third contest against which rugged overseas fighter? a) Heinz Lazek; b) Walter Neusel; c) Pierre Charles

BIG FIGHT QUIZ No 59 ANSWERS

FLOYD PATTERSON: 1. North Carolina; 2. Middle-weight; 3. Seventeen; 4. Cus D'Amato; 5. Joey Maxim; 6. Tommy Jackson; 7. Chicago; 8. Tenth round; 9. 1952; 10. 64 fights; 11. 1972; 12. Pete Rademacher; 13. Sixth round; 14. Stockholm; 15. Muhammad Ali.

SCORECARD

Points:

Result:

IN THIS CORNER

Sugar Ray Robinson

Award yourself a points win if you get seven or more right. It's a draw if you get six right. You win by a knockout if you get 11 or more right.

In which American city was Ray Robinson born?
a) Philadelphia; b) Chicago; c) Detroit

What was his name before he became a professional boxer?
a) Walker Smith; b) Virgil Jones; b) Marcus Brown

At what weight was he a Golden Gloves champion the year before turning professional? a) Featherweight; b) Light-weight; c) Welterweight

Who was his manager during his peak years as a world champion? a) Jack Hurley; b) Gil Clancy; c) George Gain-ford

Who did he outpoint for the vacant world welterweight championship? a) Chuck Taylor; b) Bernard Dicusen; c) Tommy Bell

Against which outstanding Cuban fighter did he retain the world welterweight title? a) Kid Gavilan; b) Carlos Malacara; c) Pablo Roca

Where in London did he lose the world middleweight title to Randolph Turpin? a) Wembley Arena; b) Harringay Arena; c) Earls Court

Where in New York did he regain the world title from Randolph Turpin? a) Yankee Stadium; b) Madison Square Garden; c) Polo Grounds

 In which year did he make his professional debut?
a) 1940; b) 1942; c) 1944

 How many professional fights did he have?
a) 182; b) 192; c) 202

 In which round did he knock out Rocky Graziano?
a) First; Second; c) Third

 What forced him to retire when challenging Joey Maxim for the world light-heavyweight title? a) Broken hand; b) Heat exhaustion; c) Cut eye

 How many times did Robinson win the world middleweight title? a) Three times; b) Four times; c) Five times

 Which British champion outpointed him in his only fight in Scotland? a) Pat McAteer; b) Mick Leahy; c) John McCormack

 How old was he when he lost his final contest on points to Joey Archer? a) 40; b) 42; c) 44

BIG FIGHT QUIZ No 60 ANSWERS

JACK PETERSEN: 1. Cardiff; 2. Light-heavyweight; 3. Ten months; 4. Harry Crossley; 5. Seven weeks; 6. Second round; 7. Jack Pettifer; 8. Jack Doyle; 9. 1931; 10. 38 fights; 11. 1937; 12. 13th round; 13. Len Harvey; 14. Leicester; 15. Walter Neusel.

SCORECARD

Points:

Result:

THE BIG FIGHT QUIZ No. 62

IN THIS CORNER

Max Schmeling

Award yourself a points win if you get six or more right. It's a draw if you get five right. You win by a knockout if you get 10 or more right.

 1 Where in Germany was Max Schmeling born?
a) Kassel; b) Brandenburg; c) Dusseldorf

 2 What was his popular ring nickname?
a) The Black Uhlan; b) Der Bomber; c) Kaiser Max

 3 In which weight division did he make his professional debut? a) Middleweight; b) Light-heavyweight; c) Heavyweight

 4 From whom did he take the European light-heavyweight championship? a) Fernand Delarge; b) Louis Clement; c) Michele Bonaglia

 5 Which British-based fighter stopped him in two rounds in Cologne? a) Ben Foord; b) Reggie Meen; c) Larry Gains

 6 Which British-based fighter stopped him in one round in Frankfurt? a) Gipsy Daniels; b) Tom Berry; c) Jack Bloomfield

 7 Who did he beat for the vacant world heavyweight championship in New York? a) Primo Carnera; b) Jack Sharkey; c) James J. Braddock

 8 In which round did he win the championship on a disqualification? a) Fourth round; b) Sixth round; c) Eighth round

132

In which year did he make his professional debut?
a) 1924; b) 1926; c) 1928

 How many professional fights did he have?
a) 60; b) 70; c) 80

 In which year did he have his final fight?
a) 1940; b) 1944; c) 1948

 Who did he stop in 15 rounds in his first defence of the world title? a) Mickey Walker; b) Paolino Uzcudun; c) Young Stribling

 In which round did he knock out Joe Louis in a non-title fight after losing the championship? a) Eighth round; b) Tenth round; c) Twelfth round

 Where were both his fights with Joe Louis staged?
a) Chicago; b) New York City; c) San Francisco

 He was wounded during the war while serving as a what?
a) A submariner; b) A tank commander; c) A paratrooper

THE BIG FIGHT QUIZ No. 63

IN THIS CORNER

Tony Sibson

Award yourself a points win if you get seven or more right. It's a draw if you get six right. You win by a knockout if you get 11 or more right.

1 In which Midlands city was he born and raised?
a) Leicester; b) Nottingham; c) Coventry

2 With which amateur club was he an outstanding prospect when he gained his Young England honours? a) Clifton; b) Warley; c) Belgrave

3 On which birthday did he make his professional debut?
a) Seventeenth; b) Eighteenth; c) Nineteenth

4 Who ended his 25-fight unbeaten record with a first round knockout victory? a) Pat Thomas; b) Roy Gumbs; c) Lottie Mwale

5 In which round did he stop Frankie Lucas to win the vacant British middleweight championship? a) First round; b) Third round; c) Fifth round

6 To whom did he lose the title on a points decision in his first defence? a) Kevin Finnegan; b) Bunny Sterling; c) Mark Rowe

7 Who did he outpoint to win the vacant Commonwealth middleweight title? a) Ayub Kalule; b) Chisanda Mutti; c) Monty Betham

8 In which round did he stop Matteo Salvemini to win the European middleweight championship? a) Seventh round; b) Ninth round; c) Eleventh round

134

In which year did he make his professional debut? a) 1972; b) 1974; c) 1976

 Where did he stop Alan Minter? a) Birmingham; b) Wembley; c) Manchester

 How many professional contests did he have? a) 51; b) 61; c) 71

 Where did he retain his European middleweight title with a points win against Andoni Amana? a) Naples; b) Bilbao; c) Marseilles

 In which round was he stopped when challenging Marvin Hagler for the world middleweight title? a) Fourth round; b) Sixth round; c) Eighth round

 Who did he outpoint in 1984 to regain the British and Commonwealth middleweight titles? a) Mark Kaylor; b) Herol Graham; c) Jimmy Batten

 Where was he stopped by Dennis Andries when he challenged for the world light-heavyweight title? a) Muswell Hill; b) Luton; c) Shoreditch

BIG FIGHT QUIZ No 62 ANSWERS

MAX SCHMELING: 1. Brandenburg; 2. The Black Uhlan; 3. Middleweight; 4. Fernand Delarge; 5. Larry Gains; 6. Gipsy Daniels; 7. Jack Sharkey; 8. Fourth round; 9. 1924; 10. 70 fights; 11. 1948; 12. Young Stribling; 13. Twelfth; 14. New York; 15. A paratrooper.

THE BIG FIGHT QUIZ No. 64

IN THIS CORNER
Michael Spinks

Award yourself a points win if you get seven or more right. It's a draw if you get six right. You win by a knockout if you get 11 or more right.

1 In which American state was Michael Spinks born?
a) Mississippi; b) Maryland; c) Missouri

2 At which weight did he win an Olympic gold medal?
a) Middleweight; b) Light-heavyweight; c) Heavyweight

3 Which British-born opponent did he outpoint on his way to the world title? a) Tim Woods; b) Johnny Waldron; c) Murray Sutherland

4 How many professional fights did he have before winning the WBA world light-heavyweight championship? a) 14; b) 16; c) 18

5 Who did he beat in a supporting fight on the night his brother Leon took the world title from Ali? a) Tom Bethea; b) Eddie Phillips; c) Johnny Wilburn

6 Which ex-champion did he beat to set up a fight for the WBA world light-heavyweight title? a) Mate Parlov; b) Mike Rossman; c) Marvin Johnson

7 From whom did he take the WBA light-heavyweight title?
a) Miguel Cuello; b) Mustafa Muhammad; c) Victor Galindez

8 In which round did he stop Vonzell Johnson in his first defence of the championship? a) Seventh round; b) Ninth round; c) Eleventh round

In which year did he make his professional debut?
a) 1976; b) 1977; c) 1978

 In which year did he fight Mike Tyson? a) 1987; 1988; c) 1989

 How many fights did he have before the Tyson defeat? a) 31; b) 33; c) 35

 Who did he outpoint for the undisputed world light-heavyweight title? a) Johnny Davis; b) Dwight Braxton; c) Jim MacDonald

 Where were both his title fights against Larry Holmes staged? a) Atlantic City; b) New York City; c) Las Vegas

 Against which European did he defend the world heavyweight title? a) Anders Eklund; b) Lucien Rodriguez; c) Steffan Tangstad

 How many seconds did he last against Mike Tyson? a) 71 seconds; b) 81 seconds; c) 91 seconds

BIG FIGHT QUIZ No 63 ANSWERS

SCORECARD

Points:

Result:

THE BIG FIGHT QUIZ No. 65

IN THIS CORNER

John H. Stracey

Award yourself a points win if you get seven or more right. It's a draw if you get six right. You win by a knockout if you get 11 or more right.

1 In which district of London was John H. Stracey born and raised? a) Streatham; b) Bethnal Green; c) Blackfriars

2 At which weight was he an ABA champion? a) Lightweight; b) Light-welterweight; c) Welterweight

3 What does the initial 'H' stand in John 'H' Stracey? a) Harold; b) Herbert; c) Henry

4 Which future world champion knocked him out in one round when they were amateurs? a) Jim Watt; b) Maurice Hope; c) Alan Minter

5 How was he beaten when he made his first challenge for the British welterweight title? a) On a disqualification; b) On a broken ankle; c) On a cut eye

6 Who did he stop in four rounds in a return fight for the British title? a) Pat Thomas; b) Vic Andretti; c) Bobby Arthur

7 Where did he challenge Roger Menetrey for the European welterweight championship? a) Zurich; b) Paris; c) Brussels

8 In which round did he stop Menetrey to become European champion? a) Eighth round; b) Tenth round; c) Twelfth round

138

In which year did he turn professional?
a) 1969; b) 1969; c) 1971

 How many professional fights did he have?
a) 41; b) 51; c) 61

 In which year did he have his final fight?
a) 1978; b) 1980; c) 1982

 In which round was he knocked down before getting up to take the world title from Jose Napoles? a) First round; b) Second round; c) Third round

 Who did he stop in 10 rounds in his first defence of the world title? a) Jose Palacios; b) Harold Weston; c) Hedgemon Lewis

 Where did he lose the world welterweight title to Carlos Palomino? a) Wembley Arena; b) Earls Court; c) Royal Albert Hall

 In which round was he stopped by Dave Green in their non-title showdown? a) Ninth round; b) Tenth round; c) Eleventh round

BIG FIGHT QUIZ No 64 ANSWERS

MICHAEL SPINKS: 1. Missouri; 2. Middleweight; 3. Murray Sutherland; 4. 16 fights; 5. Tom Bethea; 6. Marvin Johnson; 7. Mustafa Muhammad; 8. Seventh; 9. 1977; 10. 1988; 11. 31 fights; 12. Dwight Braxton; 13. Las Vegas; 14. Steffan Tangstad; 15. 91 seconds.

SCORECARD

Points:

Result:

THE BIG FIGHT QUIZ No. 66

IN THIS CORNER

Dick Tiger

Award yourself a points win if you get seven or more right. It's a draw if you get six right. You win by a knockout if you get 11 or more right.

1. In which country was Dick Tiger born and raised?
a) Ghana; b) Uganda; c) Nigeria

2. What was his name before he became a professional boxer?
a) Richard Coco; b) Richard Ihetu; b) Richard Bolaji

3. Where was he based during his three-year spell in England?
a) Manchester; b) Leicester; c) Liverpool

4. In which round did he stop Terry Downes in what was Terry's third professional contest? a) Fourth round; b) Sixth round; c) Eighth round

5. Who did he stop in nine rounds to win the British middleweight title? a) Phil Edwards; b) Billy Ellaway; c) Pat McAteer

6. From whom did he take the WBA world middleweight title in 1962? a) Carmen Basilio; b) Gene Fullmer; c) Sugar Ray Robinson

7. Where did he lose the world title to Joey Giardello?
a) Atlantic City; b) Lagos; c) Kampala

8. Who took the title off him after he had regained it from Joey Giardello? a) Paul Pender; b) Nino Benvenuti; c) Emile Griffith

140

In which year did he make his professional debut?
a) 1952; b) 1954; c) 1956

 How many professional fights did he have?
a) 71; b) 81; c) 91

 In which year did he make his final ring appearance?
a) 1966; b) 1968; c) 1970

 How many times did he meet his fierce rival Joey Giardello?
a) Three times; b) Four times; c) Five times

 Where did he take the world light-heavyweight title from Jose Torres? a) Puerto Rico; b) New York City; c) Mexico City

 Who did he stop in 12 rounds in defence of his light-heavyweight title? a) Roger Rouse; b) Mark Tessman; c) Vicente Rondon

 How old was he when he lost the light-heavyweight title to Bob Foster? a) 34; b) 36; c) 38

BIG FIGHT QUIZ No 65 ANSWERS

JOHN H. STRACEY: 1. Bethnal Green; 2. Light-welterweight; 3. Henry; 4. Jim Watt; 5. Disqualification; 6. Bobby Arthur; 7. Paris; 8. Eighth round; 9. 1969; 10. 51 fights; 11. 1978; 12. First round; 13. Hedgemon Lewis; 14. Wembley Arena; 15. Tenth round.

SCORECARD

Points:

Result:

THE BIG FIGHT QUIZ No. 67

IN THIS CORNER
Gene Tunney

Award yourself a points win if you get six or more right. It's a draw if you get five right. You win by a knockout if you get 10 or more right.

1 In which city in the United States was Gene Tunney born? a) Boston; b) Los Angeles; c) New York City

2 What was his popular ring nickname? a) Two-Ton Tunney; b) Sweet-As-Honey Tunney; c) The Fighting Marine

3 In which weight division did he make his professional debut? a) Middleweight; b) Light-heavyweight; c) Heavyweight

4 Where did he win the Expeditionary Force championship during the last months of World War I? a) Brussels; b) London; c) Paris

5 What rank did he hold when serving in the US Navy during World War II? a) Captain; b) Lieutenant; c) Commander

6 From which former world champion did he take the US light-heavyweight title? a) Jack Dillon; b) Jack O'Brien; c) Battling Levinsky

7 Who was the only man to conquer him and whom he subsequently beat four times? a) Harry Greb; b) Tommy Gibbons; c) Tommy Loughran

8 In which round did he stop Georges Carpentier in a non-title fight in New York City? a) Eleventh round; b) Thirteenth round; c) Fifteenth round

142

In which year did he make his professional debut?
a) 1915; b) 1917; c) 1919

 How many professional fights did he have?
a) 63; b) 73; c) 83

 In which year did he have his final fight?
a) 1928; b) 1930; c) 1932

 Who did he knock out in two rounds in his final fight before becoming world champion? a) Jimmy Delaney; b) Johnny Risko; c) Dan O'Dowd

 Where did he challenge Jack Dempsey in their first world heavyweight title fight? a) Philadelphia; b) Chicago; c) Jersey City

 What was the nationality of Tom Heeney, who challenged him for the world title in his final fight? a) Irish; b) Canadian; c) New Zealander

 In which round did he stop Heeney before announcing his retirement from boxing? a) Seventh round; b) Ninth round; c) Eleventh round

SCORECARD

Points:

Result:

IN THIS CORNER

Randolph Turpin

Award yourself a points win if you get six or more right. It's a draw if you get five right. You win by a knockout if you get 10 or more right.

1 In which Midlands county was Randolph Turpin born and raised? a) Leicestershire; b) Nottinghamshire; c) Warwickshire

2 At which weight did he win the first of his two ABA championships? a) Light-welterweight; b) Welterweight; c) Light-middleweight

3 What was his most popular ring nickname? a) The Midlands Assassin; b) The Tornado; c) The Leamington Licker

4 Who was the only British-born opponent to beat him? a) Mark Hart; b) Vince Hawkins; b) Albert Finch

5 In which round did he knock out Luc Van Dam to win the vacant European middleweight title? a) First round; b) Second round; c) Third round

6 Who was his manager throughout the peak years of his career? a) Ted Broadribb; b) Don Simpson; c) George Middleton

7 Which referee raised his hand at the end of his first world title fight against Ray Robinson? a) Mickey Fox; b) Jack Hart; c) Eugene Henderson

8 In which round was he stopped by Robinson in the return title fight? a) Tenth round; b) Twelfth round; c) Fourteenth round

In which year did he make his professional debut?
a) 1944; b) 1946; c) 1948

 How long did his reign last as world champion? a) 54 days; b) 64 days; c) 74 days

 How many professional contests did he have?
a) 75; b) 85; c) 95

 Who outpointed him for the vacant world middleweight title? a) Charles Humez; b) Carl Olson; c) Gene Fullmer

 In which round was he beaten by Tiberio Mitri when defending his European middleweight title in Rome? a) First round; b) Second round; c) Third round

 Which light-heavyweight rival did he beat three times in the late stages of his career? a) Don Cockell; b) Yolande Pompey; c) Alex Buxton

 Where did he stop Charles Seguna in two rounds in the final fight of his career? a) Gibraltar; b) Majorca; c) Malta

BIG FIGHT QUIZ No 67 ANSWERS

GENE TUNNEY: 1. New York City; 2. The Fighting Marine; 3. Middleweight; 4. Paris; 5. Commander; 6. Battling Levinsky; 7. Harry Greb; 8. Fifteenth; 9. 1915; 10. 83 fights; 11. 1928; 12. Dan O'Dowd; 13. Philadelphia; 14. New Zealander; 15. Eleventh round.

SCORECARD

Points:

Result:

IN THIS CORNER

Mike Tyson

Award yourself a points win if you get eight or more right. It's a draw if you get seven right. You win by a knockout if you get 12 or more right.

1 In which district of New York City was Mike Tyson born? a) Brooklyn; b) The Bronx; c) Queens

2 Who outpointed him in the US Olympic trials? a) Craig Payne; b) Henry Tillman; c) Al Evans

3 Who discovered him and was his early mentor? a) Angelo Dundee; b) Ace Miller; c) Cus D'Amato

4 Which former world handball champion was his co-manager at the start of his career? a) Bill Cayton; b) Jim Jacobs; c) Bobby Stewart

5 Who was the first professional opponent to take him the full distance? a) James Tillis; b) Mitch Green; c) Jose Ribalta

6 Where did he challenge Trevor Berbick for the WBC version of the world heavyweight title? a) Atlantic City; b) Los Angeles; c) Las Vegas

7 In which round did he stop Berbick in their championship contest? a) First; b) Second; c) Third

8 Who did he beat for the WBA title in his first fight after beating Berbick? a) Tim Witherspoon; b) Greg Page; c) James Smith

In which year did he make his professional debut?
a) 1983; b) 1984; c) 1985

 How old was he when he won his first world title?
a) 20; b) 21; c) 22

 How many fights did he have before beating Berbick? a) 23; b) 25; c) 27

 Where did he defend the heavyweight title against Tony Tubbs? a) Tokyo; b) Seoul; c) Osaka

 Who did he beat to become the undisputed heavyweight champion of the world? a) Michael Spinks; b) Larry Holmes; c) Tony Tucker

 In which round did he knock out Pinklon Thomas in a title defence? a) Second round; b) Fourth round; c) Sixth round

 Who refereed his title defence against British hero Frank Bruno in Las Vegas? a) Richard Steele; b) Mills Lane; c) Tony Perez

BIG FIGHT QUIZ No 68 ANSWERS

RANDOLPH TURPIN: 1. Warwickshire; 2. Welterweight; 3. The Leamington Licker; 4. Albert Finch; 5. First round; 6. George Middleton; 7. Eugene Henderson; 8. Tenth; 9. 1946; 10. 64 days; 11. 75; 12. Carl Olson; 13. First round; 14. Alex Buxton; 15. Malta.

SCORECARD

Points:

Result:

IN THIS CORNER

Jersey Joe Walcott

Award yourself a points win if you get six or more right. It's a draw if you get seven right. You win by a knockout if you get 10 or more right.

1 What was Jersey Joe Walcott's name before he started professional boxing? a) Arnold Cream; b) Alvin Jelley; c) Amos Custer

2 How old was he when he made his professional debut? a) Fifteen; b) Sixteen; c) Seventeen

3 What nationality was the original Joe Walcott, whose name Jersey Joe adopted? a) Canadian; b) West Indian; c) Cuban

4 How many years had he been a professional before becoming world heavyweight champion? a) Seventeen; b) Nineteen; c) Twenty-one

5 How old was he when he finally became heavyweight champion of the world? a) Thirty-five; b) Thirty-seven; c) Thirty-nine

6 Which future world light-heavyweight champion did he beat to earn a title shot at Joe Louis? a) Joey Maxim; b) Archie Moore; c) Bob Olin

7 Where did he make both his championship challenges against Joe Louis? a) Chicago; b) Detroit; c) New York City

8 In which round did Louis knock him out in their return contest? a) Ninth round; b) Eleventh round; c) Thirteenth round

148

In which year did he turn
professional?
a) 1926; b) 1928; c) 1930

 How many recorded
fights did he have?
a) 69; b) 79; c) 89

 In which year did he have
his final fight?
a) 1951; b) 1953; c) 1955

 How many times did he beat Ezzard Charles in their four title
fights? a) Once; b) Twice; c) Three times

 Where in Europe did he stop Olle Tandberg in five rounds?
a) Copenhagen; b) Amsterdam; c) Stockholm

 Which referee counted him out in his world title defence
against Rocky Marciano? a) Charley Daggert; b) Zack
Clayton; c) Frank Sikora

 In which round was he knocked out by Marciano in their
return world title fight? a) First round; b) Second round;
c) Third round

BIG FIGHT QUIZ No 69 ANSWERS

MIKE TYSON: 1. Brooklyn; 2. Henry Tillman; 3.
Cus D'Amato; 4. Jim Jacobs; 5. James Tillis; 6. Las
Vegas; 7. Second round; 8. James Smith; 9. 1985; 10.
20 years old; 11. 27 fights; 12. Tokyo; 13. Tony
Tucker; 14. Sixth round; 15. Richard Steele.

SCORECARD

Points:

Result:

IN THIS CORNER

Jim Watt

Award yourself a points win if you get seven or more right. It's a draw if you get six right. You win by a knockout if you get 11 or more right.

 1 In which Scottish city was Jim Watt born and raised? a) Edinburgh; b) Glasgow; c) Dundee

 2 At which weight was he an ABA champion before turning professional? a) Featherweight; b) Lightweight; c) Light-welterweight

 3 What job did he hold down during the early years of his professional career? a) Electrician; b) Mechanic; c) Plumber

 4 Who was his manager when he first won the British lightweight championship? a) Peter Keenan; b) Jim Murray; c) Paddy Byrne

 5 Who was his manager when he became the world lightweight champion? a) Dennie Mancini; b) Andy Smith; c) Terry Lawless

 6 In which round did Willie Reilly stop him with a cut eye when he first tried to win the British lightweight title? a) Sixth; b) Eighth; c) Tenth

 7 Who did he stop in 12 rounds to win the vacant British title? a) Tony Riley; b) Johnny Cheshire; c) Jimmy Revie

 8 Where did he fight Jonathan Dele for the vacant Commonwealth lightweight title? a) Kampala; b) Lagos; c) Accra

In which year did he make his professional debut?
a) 1966; b) 1967 c) 1968

 How many professional fights did he have?
a) 46; b) 56; c) 66

 In which year did he make his final ring appearance?
a) 1979; b) 1980; c) 1981

 Who did he beat for the vacant WBC world lightweight title?
a) Alfredo Pitalua; b) Robert Vasquez; c) Sean O'Grady

 In which round did he stop Charlie Nash in defence of his world title ? a) Second round; b) Fourth round; c) Sixth round

 At which football ground did he outpoint former Olympic champion Howard Davis in a title defence? a) Hampden Park; b) Ibrox; c) Parkhead

 Against whom did he make his fifth and final world title defence? a) Alexis Arguello; b) Ernesto Espana; c) Hilmer Kenty

SCORECARD

Points:

Result:

IN THIS CORNER

Jimmy Wilde

Award yourself a points win if you get six or more right. It's a draw if you get five right. You win by a knockout if you get 10 or more right.

In which town in Wales was Jimmy Wilde born and raised?
a) Tylorstown; b) Tonypandy; c) Aberdare

Apart from 'The Ghost with a Hammer in his Hand', what was his popular ring nickname? a) Mighty Midget; b) Tiny Terror; c) Mighty Atom

What was the most he weighed during his career?
a) 7st. 10lb.; b) 8st. 1lb.; c) 8st. 4lb.

In which branch of the armed forces did he serve as a physical training instructor during his career? a) Navy; b) Army; c) Flying Corps

Who defeated him in 17 rounds in his first challenge for the British flyweight title? a) Percy Jones; b) Billy Ladbury; c) Tancy Lee

He was recognised as world champion after stopping which British rival in 12 rounds? a) Joe Symonds; b) George Clark; c) Dick Heasman

In which round did he stop Tancy Lee when they met for the world title in London ? a) Eleventh round; b) Thirteenth round; c) Fifteenth round

Where did he beat Young Zulu Kid for the second time after knocking him out in London? a) Australia; b) South Africa; c) Canada

In which year did he make his professional debut?
a) 1909; b) 1911; c) 1913

 How many recorded fights did he have?
a) 153; b) 163; c) 173

 In which year did he have his final fight?
a) 1919; b) 1921; c) 1923

 How many times did he defend the world flyweight title?
a) Six times; b) Eight times; c) Ten times

 Which American stopped him in 17 rounds when Wilde was conceding a stone in weight? a) Fidel La Barba; b) Pete Herman; c) Joe Lynch

 He came out of retirement to defend his world title against which opponent? a) Pancho Villa; b) Izzy Schwartz; c) Johnny McCoy

 Where in New York did he lose his title in the final fight of his career? a) Madison Square Garden; b) Yankee Stadium; c) Polo Grounds

THE BIG FIGHT QUIZ No. 73

IN THIS CORNER

Howard Winstone

Award yourself a points win if you get seven or more right. It's a draw if you get six right. You win by a knockout if you get 11 or more right.

 1 In which area of Wales was Howard Winstone born and raised? a) Ebbw Vale; b) Carmarthen; c) Merthyr Tydfil

 2 At which weight did he win a Commonwealth Games gold medal? a) Bantamweight; b) Featherweight; c) Lightweight

 3 Which former British champion was his manager? a) Cliff Curvis; b) Eddie Thomas; c) Wally Thom

 4 From whom did he take the British featherweight championship? a) Terry Spinks; b) Bobby Neill; c) Charlie Hill

 5 In which round did he stop Derry Treanor in his first defence of the title? a) Tenth round; b) Twelfth round; c) Fourteenth round

 6 Which Scot did he outpoint to win a second Lonsdale Belt outright? a) John O'Brien; b) Johnny Morrissey; c) Chic Brogan

 7 Where did he stop fellow-Welshman Lennie Williams in a sixth successful defence of the British title? a) Llanelli; b) Porthcawl; c) Aberavon

 8 From whom did he take the European featherweight title? a) Alberto Serti; b) Olli Maeki; c) Gracieux Lamperti

154

In which year did he make his professional debut?
a) 1958; b) 1960; c) 1962

 How many professional contests did he have?
a) 57; b) 67; c) 77

 In which year did he have his final fight?
a) 1966; b) 1968; c) 1970

 Where did he lose the first of his three world title fights against Vicente Saldivar? a) Mexico City; b) Cardiff; c) London

 In which round was he stopped with a cut eye by Saldivar in their third meeting? a) Eighth round; b) Tenth round; c) Twelfth round

 Who did he beat for the vacant world featherweight title in London? a) Mitsunori Seki; b) Paul Rojas; c) Shozo Saijyo

 Where did he lose the title to Jose Legra in the final fight of his career? a) Porthcawl; b) Barcelona; c) Birmingham

SCORECARD

Points:

Result:

THE BIG FIGHT QUIZ No. 74

IN THIS CORNER
Tim Witherspoon

Award yourself a points win if you get seven or more right. It's a draw if you get six right. You win by a knockout if you get 11 or more right.

 In which United States city was Tim Witherspoon born and raised? a) Detroit; b) Miami; c) Philadelphia

 By which nickname is he popularly known?
a) Tim the Intimidator; b) Typhoon Tim; c) Terrible Tim

 Which top-rated fighter did he outpoint to set up a world title fight against Larry Holmes? a) Mike Weaver; b) Renaldo Snipes; c) Mike Dokes

 How many professional fights did he have before challenging Holmes for the world title? a) Fifteen; b) Seventeen; c) Nineteen

 Where did he drop a disputed points decision to Holmes in their title fight? a) Las Vegas; b) Atlantic City; c) Cleveland

 Who did he stop in one round to win the North American heavyweight title? a) Marvis Frazier; b) James Tillis; c) Jimmy Young

 In which round did he stop James Broad in a North American heavyweight championship contest? a) First; b) Second; c) Third

 Who did he beat for the vacant WBC championship? a) Greg Page; b) Gerrie Coetzee; c) John Tate

156

In which year did he make his professional debut?
a) 1977; b) 1978; c) 1979

 How old was he when he won his first world title?
a) 21; b) 23; c) 25

 Who was his manager when he fought Frank Bruno? a) Jim Jacobs; b) Bill Cayton; c) Carl King

 To whom did he lose the WBC heavyweight title in his first defence? a) Pinklon Thomas; b) Trevor Berbick; c) Tony Tucker

 Where in England did he fight fellow-American Sammy Scaff? a) Manchester; b) Liverpool; c) Birmingham

 Who was the referee when he defended the WBA heavyweight title against Bruno? a) Isidro Rodriguez; b) Vincent Rainone; c) David Pearl

 To whom did he lose the WBA title when stopped in the first round? a) Tony Tubbs; b) Tyrell Biggs; c) James Smith

---

BIG FIGHT QUIZ No 73 ANSWERS

HOWARD WINSTONE: 1. Merthyr Tydfil; 2. Bantamweight; 3. Eddie Thomas; 4. Terry Spinks; 5. Fourteenth ; 6. John O'Brien; 7. Aberavon; 8. Alberto Serti; 9. 1958; 10. 67 fights; 11. 1968; 12. London; 13. Twelfth; 14. Mitsunori Seki; 15. Porthcawl.

SCORECARD

Points:

Result:

IN THIS CORNER

Bruce Woodcock

Award yourself a points win if you get six or more right. It's a draw if you get seven right. You win by a knockout if you get 10 or more right.

1 Where was Bruce Woodcock born and raised?
a) Doncaster; b) Newcastle; c) Grimsby

2 At which weight did he win an ABA title three years before turning professional? a) Middleweight; b) Light-heavyweight; c) Heavyweight

3 Who was his manager throughout his career?
a) Tom Hurst; b) George Middleton; c) Sam Burns

4 Who did he knock out in six rounds to become British and Empire heavyweight champion? a) Len Harvey; b) Eddie Phillips; c) Jack London

5 In which round did he knock out Albert Renet to win the European heavyweight championship? a) Fourth round; b) Sixth round; c) Eighth round

6 Where was he stopped in five rounds by world-rated American Tami Mauriello? a) New York City; b) Boston; c) Pittsburgh

7 Who did he outpoint in his first defence of the European title? a) Jo Weiden; b) Hein ten Hoff; c) Stephane Olek

8 What injury did he suffer in the first round against giant American Joe Baksi? a) Broken hand; b) Sprained ankle; c) Broken jaw

In which year did he turn professional?
a) 1938; b) 1940; c) 1942

 How many professional fights did he have?
a) 38; b) 40; c) 42

 In which number fight did he win the British title?
a) 19; b) 21; c) 23

 Where did he knock out Freddie Mills in 14 rounds in defence of his titles? a) White City; b) White Hart Lane; c) Harringay Arena

 In which round did he knock out Johnny Ralph in defence of his Empire title in Johannesburg? a) Third round; b) Fifth round; c) Seventh round

 Who beat him in a fight for the European version of the world title? a) Gus Lesnevich; b) Freddy Beshore; c) Lee Savold

 He retired after losing his titles to which challenger at Earls Court? a) Johnny Williams; b) Jack Gardner; c) Don Cockell

BIG FIGHT QUIZ No 74 ANSWERS

SCORECARD

Points:

Result:

THE FINAL BELL

Are you a champion?

Add all the points you have scored in the 75 big fight challenges, and then see how you rate using the score guide below.

You win by a knockout if you have totalled 700 or more points, and you can consider yourself in world championship class for all-round boxing knowledge.

You win on a stoppage if you have totalled between 600 and 699 points, and you can consider yourself in European title class for all-round boxing knowledge.

You win on points if you have totalled between 500 and 599 points, and you can consider yourself in British title class for all-round boxing knowledge.

You have been held to a draw if you have totalled between 400 and 499 points, and you have to concede defeat if you have scored less than 400 points.

BIG FIGHT QUIZ No 75 ANSWERS

BRUCE WOODCOCK: 1. Doncaster; 2. Light-heavyweight; 3. Tom Hurst; 4. Jack London; 5. Sixth round; 6. New York; 7. Stephane Olek; 8. Broken jaw; 9. 1942; 10. 40 fights; 11. 21 fights; 12. White City; 13. Seventh; 14. Lee Savold; 15. Jack Gardner.

SCORECARD

Points:

Result: